Seven Ravens

Two summers in a
life by the sea

Selected Books by Lesley Choyce

Fiction

Cold Clear Morning
Dance the Rocks Ashore
The Republic of Nothing
Sea of Tranquility
World Enough

Non-Fiction

The Coasts of Canada
Driving Minnie's Piano
Nova Scotia: Shaped By the Sea
Peggy's Cove: The Amazing History of a Coastal Village

Poetry

Beautiful Sadness
The Discipline of Ice
Caution to the Wind
Revenge of the Optimist
Typographical Eras

Seven Ravens

*Two summers in a
life by the sea*

by Lesley Choyce

Wolsak and Wynn

Cover design: Gail LeBlanc
Author's photograph: Daniel Abriel
Typeset in Minion Pro and Adobe Garamond Pro
Printed by Ball Media, Brantford, Canada

     Canadian   Patrimoine
Heritage   canadien

The publishers gratefully acknowledge the support of the Canada Council for the Arts, the Ontario Arts Council and the Book Publishing Industry Development Program (BPIDP) for their financial assistance.

Wolsak and Wynn Publishers Ltd.
#102 69 Hughson Street North
Hamilton, ON
Canada L8R 1G5

Library and Archives Canada Cataloguing in Publication

Choyce, Lesley, 1951-
Seven ravens : two summers in a life by the sea / Lesley Choyce.

ISBN 978-1-894987-39-4

1. Choyce, Lesley, 1951-. 2. Natural history--Nova Scotia.
3. Nova Scotia--Biography. 4. Authors, Canadian (English)--20th century--Biography. I. Title.

PS8555.H668Z467 2009   C818'.5409   C2009-904019-0

This book is dedicated to my parents,
George and Norma Choyce.

Contents

Introduction

This book is about a journey I took over a two-year period of my life, a journey from despair to happiness. It was prompted by a mid-life crisis of some sort but if I were to spell out the causes, I don't think you'd have much sympathy for my downfall. In retrospect, there was not that much wrong with my life, but nonetheless various unexpected and challenging changes had knocked me down several rungs on the wobbly ladder I was climbing. Suffice it to say I needed repair and, at first, I didn't have a clue about how to get the job done.

Friends and colleagues and even family weren't jumping up and down to help, probably because I didn't reveal that much of anything was wrong. I was a pro at appearing normal and even competent in most things I did. I'm a novelist, a university teacher, a publisher and a sometimes TV talk show host. In fact, I keep myself so busy from September to the end of April that I often don't have the luxury of indulging in one of my most important passions – writing. But from May to the end of August I give myself license to ponder, to meditate, to explore, to study myself and the natural world around me. And to write. And so this is the story of two summers of my life here at Lawrencetown Beach living on an old farm by the North Atlantic.

This is not the story of a young man's anxiety or an old man's grief. This is about a guy somewhere in the middle trying to pull himself back together, yet again trying to make sense out of the world.

I live on the edge of a ragged spruce forest, a stone's throw from the sea. Those summers I retreated to the forest; or to empty shorelines; or out onto the lakes, inlets and sea in canoe, kayak or on surfboard. I let nature work at my wounds. I was restored for a while and then lost ground. Like an old car, rusting away, I needed repair often.

In that dense spruce forest behind my house, a tangled, sometimes receptive chunk of forest, I purposefully wandered until I was lost because that's what I was feeling in other aspects of my life. And then I proceeded to find my way back home, taking plenty of wrong turns, stumbling at times, even clawing my way through undergrowth.

I was on a quest to reformulate my understanding of who I was and where I was going. I needed something to sustain me in spite of my recent bad luck and in spite of myself. I was certain that it was not a prescription for anti-depressants or a rigorous schedule with therapists that would help. Whatever "cure" was out there, I would have to find it on my own – or at least, I'd have to find it my way. And did.

I did not find God or the ultimate meaning of the universe. Instead I found rocks and trees and small, injured animals and some helpful books written centuries ago. I found truth – at least a satisfying version of something close to truth – while kayaking alone to islands in the Atlantic, while surfing in nearly impenetrable fog, while climbing down sheer rock face cliffs in search of amethyst and while travelling north and south, east and west.

More often than not, it was the natural things of this world that cushioned the blow to my ego now that I fully understood that I was mortal, damaged goods on a downhill slide to death. I don't know why the singing sparrow, the sway of sea oats, the sifting sand on a windswept beach and the beautiful eyes of a wild duck have such restorative powers, but they do.

There were people involved in my journey and there was adventure. In the end, there was a story, this story. The truth that was revealed to me had many faces, many facets, many particulars and no easy, single, quotable name. Yet it was there and, in the telling, I can provide all of the intimate details.

As is my nature, I was trying to write my way out of my despair along the way. I knew that things made sense once you wrote them down. Most importantly, I believed that it was my job to make connections between unlikely events and ideas. Sun Tzu accompanied me on my search for Lake No Good. Voltaire was my only ally when I found myself sitting out the fog on a slippery rock perch near the mouth of Halifax Harbour.

As a humble explorer in the twelve billion year old universe, I travelled light. But my safety net was made of many threads of learning and experience and belief. The notebook forced me to observe and connect and language provided the specific knots that allowed me to connect one thing to the next. In my knapsack, always, with the water bottle, the topographic map and the compass, were stories from my own past that could be spread out on a rocky boulder at low tide, or by the raging waterfall of Hell's Gate, or wherever I was.

Ever testing my ability to connect the most disparate subjects, I hit a few dead ends but more often I found the connection I was looking for. In the random universe, quantum physics instructs us that what seems logical may not necessarily be true and something that seems totally crazy may be the path to enlightenment – or at least to some small parcel of truth that can get you through a tough spot.

On the rocky shore near where I surf, I once saved a raven with a broken wing. He punished me well for saving him – tore open my arms with his talons, but I didn't hold a grudge. I had his wing set, named him Jack, and I kept him safe for the time it took for the wing to heal. I retrained him to fly after that and set him free. He stayed in the neighbourhood and greeted me each day for several years until a hunter killed him during goose hunting season.

Wherever I travel, I see ravens. In the woods, by the shoreline or out along the highways, whether it's here in Nova Scotia, north in Labrador, on a remote beach near Tofino on Vancouver Island or in the highlands of Scotland. Ravens and their only slightly lesser cousins, the crows, are ubiquitous in my life.

I have a belief about ravens. I can believe a thing that is or is not true, as long as it serves me in a positive way. I believe that those ravens out there know that I saved Jack from certain death and that since I did this good deed for their species, from now on, it is their job to watch out for me. To make sure I am safe.

Hence the raven at the top of the splintered white pine waiting for me at the pinnacle above the rockfall at Devil's Bed. And of course the ravens that sit on the old swing set each morning waiting for me to walk out the back door. And the ravens lining the highway even on my drive to the airport. They are all watching out for me.

And sometimes those ravens can provide a code which might help me reaffirm my sanity, provide the road map leading from chaos to order. I want to believe that it's all about something, that it all adds up to something wonderful and vibrant.

So a simple test goes like this. I will hike north from the Number Seven Highway, into the great inland expanse of wilderness that is in the middle of this province. I'll follow an overgrown trail until the forest usurps it and then continue on over hills and across streams, stopping to write in my notebook each time I see a raven. I will assure myself that something significant, something vital, will happen at each point along the way until I am seven ravens from home. And at that point, I turn around and return, retracing my steps or theorizing an alternate path back to civilization.

Ravens can fool me easily, they look so much alike. Is the same raven following me that I see seven times or a different one at each spotting? I don't know. All I know is that if I believe in the seven ravens theory, if I attune my senses to discovering what is around me and within me each time I stop, amazing things happen. Connections are made.

And if I spend enough time keeping up the search for the profound in the seemingly ordinary, the light comes back into the world and I find a cure for all of the darkness within me.

Year One

June 24

A Certain Slant of Rain

There is a certain slant of rain, a tilt of water, sheets of it, sky drool drifting and then suddenly driving down, powered by the east wind, of course – Atlantic driven, drowning us in spring. The hills sodden, the drumlins leaking dirty tears into the sea.

I was interrupted yesterday mid-paragraph, writing about life/death distinctions. It was a phone call from a friend telling me about his cancer. Sitting at my computer, at my wide chaos of a desk, the fan motor of my computer in my ears, I felt the heaviness of this world descend on me. My friend from further up the shore, a writer too, was scheduled for surgery. He seemed to talk more slowly than ever as if he'd been beaten down and I worried he was feeling depressed – like I had been, these past eighteen months. Another slant of grey rain. I asked him outright and he gave me an answer I didn't fully understand but will someday – if, or when, my turn comes.

"I can talk about it now," he said. "It's a turning point."

Then we both talked directly about death, laughed about it even. But that was on a day when the sun was still out and it was summer-warm only to be fooled by night-time sleet and the morning impregnated by grey rain.

On the weekend, my twenty-two-year-old daughter Sunyata brought home five baby red squirrels, two infant pigeons and a pair of baby rats. It was a salvation project, one of many in this household. This year, she is working for Hope Swinimer, who runs an animal rehabilitation centre in Seaforth. Hope's pet skunk, the docile, near-sighted Zorro, was a capable actor in my tongue-in-cheek documentary film, *The Skunk Whisperer*. Hope takes in injured wild animals, nurses them back to health and releases them into the wild. Some cannot be released so they stay on – human-loving raccoons, orphaned skunks, one-winged sea gulls and River, the playful, sometimes over zealous river otter.

When I arrived home from New Brunswick, I helped to feed the baby squirrels by squirting milk into their mouths from a hypodermic syringe minus the needle. The kitchen looked as if a party of heroin addicts had moved in. Syringes gathering in cereal bowls, needles set aside, still in their plastic wrapping. The squirrels were the size of thumbs and not at all afraid of me. One fell asleep in my shirt pocket while I nursed another one, training it to drink from the end of the syringe while I gently pushed the plastic plunger. I was reminded of the junkie who used to sit by me in Bryant Park in New York City. During my lunch break from graduate seminars on Jonathan Swift and John Milton, I would station myself on a park bench behind the New York Public library and eat a pair of bologna sandwiches while a young guy opened his kit, tethered his arm and slowly, carefully – religiously even – injected himself with heroin.

It was a crowded park, hard to find seating on a bench but there was always a place beside the young silent junkie, as if he were saving it for me. He wasn't there every day, but often enough, and it seemed as if this too was his lunch break from work or school and instead of food, he fuelled himself with a deadly drug. I had tried asking him questions but he never spoke more than a few syllables. Once he nodded off and his head slipped onto my shoulder as I ate and read from an essay by Jonathan Swift called

"The Mechanical Operation of the Spirit." I never knew his name and always wondered at the very public nature of his drug habit. In the end, I suppose, it either killed him or kept him alive. Maybe it was a bridge to a better place, an escape from a private hell or a matter of daily routine that got him through the day. People on the periphery of our lives come and go. Some diminish to distant vaporous wraiths. Others leave baggage behind. The junkie from Bryant Park who shared my bench reminded me a little too much of one potential self – my potential self – for him to evaporate in the mists of years. I wish him well if he is still alive.

"Whenever I find myself growing grim about the mouth... then I account it is high time to get myself to sea as soon as I can." So speaks Ishmael in the first paragraph of *Moby Dick*. I've given you the Cole's Notes version of the sentence because sandwiched between the "whenever" and the "then" is a large smattering of definition about grimness and despair.

Keeping things alive has always been a household theme here in Nova Scotia. After the cancer phone call from my friend, I felt that tightness of muscles around my mouth that Ishmael had spoken of. What I needed was not fiction but waves – surfing, to be precise. For me, it would not be necessary to send myself off on a long sea voyage with a maniacal captain in search of a white whale. An hour of surfing smooth blue Atlantic peaks would suffice but, alas, the sea was flat. Nonetheless, I walked toward the ocean on that day of rare sun. Deep in reverie, I almost stepped on a three-foot long garter snake. Still groggy with the cold season, he found the gravel road a warm place to bask in the sun. Snake brains are slow to register the danger of cars and trucks. I positioned myself behind him and pretended to be a predator, chasing him in the direction he wanted to go until he was buried in the safety of the tall grasses of the marsh.

His was the colour of the gravel road and within minutes a four-wheel drive truck trundled by. The driver would not have seen the snake. Chalk up one creature saved. Although I know that in this life, it's always a temporary victory.

R D. Laing says that when someone is psychotic, "imagination may seem to be objective reality."

The fiction writer in me can identify with this objective reality. When I can afford to, I retreat, like the New York heroin addict, to the gentle form of psychosis we call fiction. Soon enough I am summoned back to normality by a phone call about cancer or the needs of family, snakes, squirrels or baby pigeons.

The baby pigeons were much harder to feed. More syringe work was required and, oddly enough, Hope had said we should feed them cat food mixed with water. I had nursed many baby pigeons before so I knew that it required a kind of persistent forcing of food down their throats even though it felt nearly brutal, this force required to make them eat. In the old days, I would take cracked corn and pound it up with a hammer, then mix it with warm water. The pounding of hard corn with a hammer felt primitive and rewarding, I recall.

I fed the baby pigeons while watching *Star Trek: Voyager*. Data was having problems with his positronic network. Such a workable excuse for explaining a bad day would be a desirable option to explain to our colleagues why we were behaving badly.

Sunyata had spent considerable time that weekend nursing baby rats. With Hope away for the weekend, our house had become a nursery for whatever infant creatures had been stranded and rescued that week in Nova Scotia, including the baby rats, which turned out to be exceedingly cute.

Now in our household we have not had entirely good experiences with adult rats and the idea of "saving" orphaned rats was suspect by all – including Sunyata's friends. So to all except her father – she was sure I would understand why she was trying to save any living thing, even rats – she claimed they were not rats at all but moles.

The moles were very cute.

By the time I had arrived on the scene to watch *Star Trek* and feed pocket squirrels, the rats had moved on to another household where the feeders thought they were helping to save moles, not rats. I didn't know what kind of life or career the rats had ahead of them. These were not white pet store rats; these were wild, possibly Norwegian rats, the kind that chew through the insulation of wires in your attic, causing your house to burn down.

On the selfsame weekend of animal rescue, a giant grey hawk killed one of my pigeons. The same hawk, I believe, that had killed this pigeon's mother. The pigeons live outside in a cage but I rejoice on calm sunny days when I open the door and watch the pigeons fly free. They spiral higher and higher into the sky until I lose them in the sun. They swoop and flaunt the wind, scoop the air and pull themselves higher and higher into the clouds with a grace suggesting birds are more privileged than men and women. On average, every three years a predator dives from a higher altitude and impales one with talons so sharp that blood appears immediately on the smooth feathers.

The victim this time was a pigeon I had once named Darwin, although the name never stuck and, instead, he was known as simply Buddy. A hawk had attacked Darwin/Buddy once before when he was less than a year old. But Sunyata and I had both been right there when it happened. The hawk had landed nearby in a field and had not yet been able to use its deadly beak to bite into the neck of its victim. It was shocked to find a screaming banshee child and father come running through the ground juniper to the rescue. Buddy survived a good seven years beyond that but met the predator again during our wildlife salvation weekend.

I found what was left of Darwin in the woods and there was not much of him that remained. The hawk may have been a killer but he did not waste what he killed. I carried the white flight feathers home and put them in a vase.

A partial inventory of my desk reveals the following: two old eight-track tapes (Styx and Ambrosia), a myriad of books – Melville, Hemingway, desk encyclopaedias, Carl Rogers, a textbook of logic, poetry books, biographies, and a volume by R.D. Laing, who continues to tutor me about madness. There is one coffee cup with lukewarm dark roast coffee, boxes of floppy discs archiving decades of work (if this be work), a phone that works, one that doesn't. The phone that works goes dead, however, if anyone else picks up the line. There lies here also glue and glasses, notebooks, outdated video games, a leather bookmark with my name stamped into it. It appears to be made from a belt. There are unfinished novels here, some which will never be finished.

There are dreams charted out in notebooks. There is madness here too, pages written in heat and haste. There is a cap that I call my Alistair MacLeod hat. I wear it when I want to write elegiac prose like Alistair MacLeod but rarely does the hat inspire the head to come close to mimicking the master.

There is a basket of shells in the window. I recognize whelks and small conches and the shed casings of periwinkles and even a sample or two of what my daughters Sunyata and Pamela once called "magic rocks," perfectly rounded jewels of blue and green and crystal. Moulded and polished by the sea, the rocks are not rocks at all but amulets of glass, fashioned from broken bottles and once found as casual gifts on these shorelines. Ironically, during the years when my children grew, these gems diminished on these shores, as if they were a species going extinct as a direct result of major strides in recycling and environmental concern. Even that great compassion has its price and loss.

But if I root around on my desk long enough, I will find my leftover ambition from my younger years. There is dust here with the ambition and the carcasses of dead flies from a previous season and phone cords and computer cables and pages with scribbled notes I take while driving my car. I have a clipboard and when something strikes me as interesting, insightful or important, I scribble on it as I drive one-handed. One hand on the wheel, one wielding the pen. My notes often are illegible and ignored but I'm afraid of losing something if I don't write it down. In truth, I'm afraid of losing everything – and not just my mind, but my soul, perhaps. So I write it all down. Even if I can't read it later, even if I don't make use of it.

On one page, this list:

1. naked, thumbless
2. speech/language
3. eyes, beard, wound
4. who is it?
5. nothingness
6. intrepid, fearless
7. "Where are my wings?"

Beyond the clutter on my desk, the rain now hits like small bullets on my window facing south. The storm comes at me from the sea. Last evening my daughter and I watched a wolf in the marsh. He was much larger than any wolf I have seen on TV or in any wildlife park. Sunyata had seen this wolf before in the forest, and we had all doubted her reports. But there he was in full view in the moonlight – certainly larger than a German shepherd. By official accounts, such wolves should not exist in this part of the world. Perhaps the experts are somehow mistaken.

So we begin to believe that various forms of predators are on the increase. Thomas Browne in the seventeenth century wrote, "The long habit of living indisposeth us for dying." Buried still in the pile of words, books and personal history on my desk are still some shards of enthusiastic belief and even hopefulness left over from younger years. If I rummage about long enough, they too will surface and be put to good use in the days to come.

June 30

Mosquitoes by the Musquodoboit

On June 30th I sat beside the Musquodoboit River, under a large spruce tree that sheltered me from the rain that weather forecasts had failed to predict. I was disappointed that I would not be hiking to the cliffs on Pace's Lake – the goal that brought me here. But I had a river and a tree and a book for cross-referencing my own thoughts. And I had a 50/50 split of black flies and mosquitoes. And a possible title for a chapter: "Mosquitoes by the Musquodoboit" (pronounced Musk-cod-dob-bit), a Mi'kmaq word or a corruption of one meaning "rolling out in foam." Somewhere below here, the river itself tumbled through a narrow canyon and out into a bay. It did roll out with dark water topped by thick white foam which reminded me of the exact same pairing of colours and textures I'd once seen in a glass of Guinness poured straight and slowly from the tap in a little pub in Doolin on the west coast of Ireland.

But it was too early in the day to be thinking about Guinness, and Ireland was on the other side of the ocean. As I sat on my pack and fixed the bug hood over my head – a first, since I'd never written hooded and veiled – I decided to take notes of my thoughts and read from my book and not worry about the rain or bugs. I discovered I was amazingly dry beneath the shelter of the large pine, as the black flies bumped into the protective netting round my head. I put on my glasses – my old one-dollar pair of black-rimmed Buddy Holly glasses. I put them on outside of the mesh and realized that this didn't quite work, so I put them inside and now of course I realized the entire world looked different. Not only was everything beyond reading distance a blur but also a blur with a fine mesh that gave everything the texture of one of those slightly out of focus old paintings by a European master.

Everything around me was green and lush and now slightly out of focus and textured by the veil. Now I was getting somewhere.

Like every other fool on the planet I am in this constant game of self-discovery. I'm not very good at it but I'm at least open-minded and willing to learn from whatever comes my way. Today I could not shinny up the gully at the edge of a cliff and there was no surf for surfing and all of my sense of adventure was failing me but yet I had my tree, book, notebook, rain and bugs to work with – which was potentially more than enough. I also had the "scheduled river" alongside of me.

There was a plastic sign posted to the tree behind me that read, "This is a scheduled river and from _____ to _____ no person shall fish by any means other than artificial fly, within the limits of the waters as follows_____

_____
_____."

There was no information completed for the "to" and "from" part and none after "follows" although you could see a faint tracing of someone's magic marker that had not been waterproof, so the warning was ambiguous. The next section sounded as if Izaak Walton had replaced the author perhaps.

"No person shall angle in these waters during the dates mentioned above [the blank ones] from 10:00 o'clock in the afternoon Local Time until 6:00 o'clock in the forenoon Local Time of the following day."

I truly liked the verb, "angle," and I assume it means to fish with those wavy lines swishing backwards and forwards like the guys did in the movie *A River Runs Through It*, although I could never figure out how you actually catch a fish waving the fishing line around in the breeze. But angling – my own version of angling – is what I was doing here, not fishing; the fish deserved to stay there wet and lovely in their Musquodoboit home. I was angling – fishing for ideas, but also angling in the other respect: coming at something obliquely, not directly.

I also wondered about "10:00 o'clock in the afternoon." My afternoon ended at about five and sometimes it stretched out until six but apparently, among anglers, it cruised right on until ten o'clock. Many nights I'm in bed by ten o'clock. I call it night and not afternoon. It was a totally different way of looking at the world – but you were not allowed to fish here after that and could not get back at it until six o'clock in the forenoon rolled around.

"It is unlawful to use in the aforementioned waters during the aforementioned dates any bait, lure, spinning device, or any added weight for the purpose of causing a fly to sink."

I wondered if certain worms were legal, others not. Was there a black market for illegal worms? Or flies. And I couldn't quite picture a "spinning device." I'm sure it referred to some kind of fishing reel but, instead, I pictured a fantastic convoluted machine that anglers would haul out into the Musquodoboit River and spin in – human spinning devices that would twirl them around – a kind of centrifuge thing like astronauts would use to practice for a crisis in space. This spinning machine would confuse the fish and make them too easy to catch, thus reducing the fish population.

"Persons who violate the above conditions will be prosecuted accordingly." The sign was signed by someone who simply referred to his generic self as "Canada Fisheries and Oceans."

As the rain diminished to a dribble and then promptly started up again, I pondered how one was "prosecuted accordingly." My reading of that implied that if you used lead weights, what we used to call "sinkers," you would be dropped into deep water yourself with lead weights on. That's what "accordingly" meant in my book. Illegal worms? How would you be punished for using the wrong worms? Illegal bait? Spinning device? Prison, I suppose for such offenses on a scheduled river.

The sign had one final footnote to deal with anyone angered by the rules or weird language: "Persons damaging this sign will be prosecuted."

Just suppose someone arrived here to fish and he or she was doing everything wrong. He arrived at five in the forenoon and he was not on schedule with the river. He had worms, and bacon bits and dragonflies for bait. Perhaps he had shiny platinum lures that his Uncle Phil had made and sold over the Internet. He had spectacular spinning devices dreamed up by renegade Rand Corporation think tank geniuses and he had ten pounds of lead to sink his hooks into the river whenever he damned well pleased. Suppose he had all this and the sign angered him and he tore the sign down.

And suppose that just then a fisheries officer was pulling up for a forenoon check to make sure that no one was messing with the river schedule.

We are probably talking about life imprisonment.

I couldn't help but nail a couple of mosquitoes drawing blood from my right hand and then wondered, why were they assaulting only the right hand? Was it because that one was associated with the left side of my brain, the logic centre of my mind? They didn't mess with my left hand, the one associated with my right lobe, my potent irrational, creative side. No, they didn't want to mess with all that power. So they tried to suck the logic out of me until my right hand stopped writing and I used my thumb to kill them – but only the ones who bit, not the tourist mosquitoes that simply landed and saw that I was writing and flew off to seek the blood of the lawyers who had written the sign. I, of course, hurled (an exaggerated verb perhaps) the carcasses of the dead mosquitoes into the river for the frogs or fish or whatever – thereby, undoubtedly violating the law by tempting the fish with something that was not an "artificial fly." But I didn't care.

My intention was not to get sidetracked by the tacky, confused and partitioned aspects of human life. After all, on my ride here I was listening to an audio book. Shirley MacLaine was walking the Camino in Spain and, as far as I could tell, she was just walking down a long but interesting path in the tradition of other pilgrims. I liked the stuff about the walking stick "choosing her" and about the problem with dogs and reporters. Like Ms. MacLaine, I was on my own pilgrimage.

Driving along the rainy Musquodoboit, Shirley had spoken to me about her dreams or visions or whatever they were and she was suddenly back in Atlantis and before that a place called Lamoria. She spoke of a time when humans were androgynous and visited by aliens who were trying to help us along with our evolution. And they had crystals and telepathy and back-and-forth energy transfers between souls and she had a memory that stretched that far back. And then some bad shit happened and these humans who were our forefather/mothers (sort of in the forenoon of humanity on the scheduled river of time) "fell from grace" and got hooked on individuality and attachment to material things and ideas.

I had stopped at the Tim Hortons in Porters Lake on the way here and only three people were inside sitting at tables. All the other customers – twenty of them looking like protestors because they seemed to be blocking the entrance to Tim's – were standing out in the thin drizzle, smoking and coughing while they drank large coffees. I went inside with the non-smokers and ordered a small coffee to go and drove on toward Musquodoboit Harbour with Shirley MacLaine telling me about another of her past lives where she was a "Moorish girl" who cured a potentate of his impotence by creating the right vibrations for him.

It didn't take long for the small caffeine euphoria of Tim Hortons coffee and listening to a wild (but intriguing!) audio book to kick in. I took a break from Shirley's story because she kept angling off the Camino and into her visionary past and I wanted to hear about her hike. I should probably admit that I'm a fan of her ideas even if I don't necessarily believe them. I think some of the stuff is funny. But I do think people can be cured by the right vibrations – or at least turned on by them. She was arguing that sex was so powerful because it was all tied in with God and divine spirit and I say, why not?

Now, sitting beneath the tree, chiding myself for letting my ego get in the way of my happiness and my loss of enthusiasm, I let the writing and the whole atmosphere work on me. I had had my fun with the fishing sign – oh, so much more complicated than the old ones that once said "No Fishing." You either could or you couldn't fish in the days of my youth. The river had no schedules then when I was a boy who caught catfish, using sinkers and worms that I dug out of the ground myself.

This summer, my fifty-second, I was facing breathing problems and that made me sit and appreciate every good breath I had inside my little mesh tent around my head. I thought about surfing and how my doctor had told me to "avoid cold water," which is hard to do if you want to surf in Nova Scotia year-round.

Soon I started to feel sorry for myself, which I am prone to do, so I took a drink from my water bottle – drinking through the net of the bug hood just to see what that was like. I was filtering everything through the veil. A great white birch tree nearby was leaning over the river and its classic white bark was curling up in places like the pages of an old book left outside in the damp.

So all these things were accomplished on this day: a dissertation on the fishing sign, musings about veils and perception, and past life regression to androgyny, art appreciation and much more. I decided it was time to look for inspiration from the book in my pack: *Subtle Wisdom* by Master Sheng-Yen. The subtitle was

Understanding Suffering (which I inadvertently first scanned as "Understanding Surfing") and sub-subtitled *Cultivating Compassion Through Ch'an Buddhism*.

Master Sheng-Yen "received Dharma transmission" in two major schools of Ch'an, which turned out to be Zen or a kind of Zen, and he wrote excellent prose – real straightforward and to the point. I read about Shakyamuni, born 2600 years ago and how he got this school of Buddhism rolling along.

Drifting from the text, I got caught up in the percussion of the sound of raindrops falling on broad leaves. It was pretty good timpani until it was interrupted by a distant chainsaw. There have been a lot of distant chainsaw noises in my recent pilgrimages and I was wondering if that meant something. Up to now I thought that I had been sitting in a quiet place but realized I had the drum drops going on the trees, the light cymbal sound of rain falling uninterrupted on the Musquodoboit River, the nasal drone of mosquitoes barred from finding my head by the bug net and now the background chainsaw, a not-so-subtle reminder that man is always not far off, operating something or other that requires spark plugs and exhaust.

My leg was asleep and I thought that was one of those great Buddhist jokes or, as Shirley MacLaine might have interpreted it, as losing sensory contact with my physical self. (Go, girl!) Shakyamuni, it turned out, was an advocate of the "Middle Way" and not of extremes. I liked him immensely for coming up with the idea, "Things are just as they are." In other words, they are just as you see them, not what you want them to be or dread them to be. He further explained that there is "no need to give rise to vexations." This referred to likes and dislikes, opinion, attitudes, views, emotions, attachment. All those things led to suffering and misery.

The chainsaw suddenly stopped. Buddy was probably taking a smoke break but I was left alone with the profound music of the rain. Suddenly, things were just as they were. I was still attached to it because I liked the sound, I liked the rain, and I liked the notes

I scribbled on my notebook. But I was for the most part unvexed. I was here and now and that was the toughest thing to accomplish in any of my days. I wanted to be unvexed and this morning was my therapy, my minor enlightenment.

Master S said that you could be enlightened if you could achieve the four nos: no mind, no form, no abiding and no thought. The chainsaw started up again as smoke break ended and at first I wanted to curse the unknown tree cutter but then realized that there would always be a chainsaw in the distance so I better build it into my soundtrack. And so it was. The river was still beautiful in the rain and I thought, "I am sitting beside the river, under the tree, beside the path. This is perfect. I am off the path and sitting quietly, as close to feeling peaceful as I have been for several months. No complaining, no smoking, no speaking."

I had not achieved no-mind but there were a million things I was NOT doing and that was pretty damn good for my mental health and me. Master S told me a story about an ancient Chinese pilgrim who asked a *bhiksu* (monk) why he was meditating and the monk said it was because he was trying to "become Buddha." The pilgrim, who turned out to be more enlightened than the monk, said the monk was wasting his time: doing such a thing was "like polishing a brick, hoping to make a mirror."

The author also made the point, "What you fear is what you must confront," and of course that was bang on. So I decided to make a list of what I was afraid of: boring meetings, dull social situations, not being able to hold my breath when wiping out in the frigid North Atlantic. I would confront them one by one. But that would be for another day.

It was ten after eleven in the morning (forenoon still) when I closed my notebook, lifted the veil and returned myself to the ordinary world. Almost "nothing" (no-thing) had happened to me today but it had been a spectacular morning

On the way home, I heard Shirley MacLaine report about the end of her trek to the shrine of St. James. It all ended kind of quickly and she knew people like me were still sceptical of all the Atlantis androgyny stuff so she did well to remind me as I was driving through Musquodoboit Harbour (past a sign that said "The Harbour Barber") that "The absence of evidence does not mean the evidence of absence."

July 4

I Decide to Become a Shaman

Here on one of my darker days of the year I have decided to be a shaman, thanks to a book that I am reading called *So You Want to Be a Shaman*. It's a really good little book for such a sad, damp day and I will use small parts of this book to heal myself as best I can.

I have already made a promise that I will not take my role lightly or use my shamanism, if I succeed in my apprenticeship, for purely selfish purposes.

Imagine being able to walk into a bookstore and buy a book for $1.98 (a clearance item) that may turn a person into a shaman. I think this *is* possible because my shamanistic side already believes that most (well, almost all) things are possible. This is an old axe I've been grinding away at for years: if you think you can do a thing, you probably can and if you really can't, then pretend you can anyway.

The first thing I understand is that shamans need to be aware of stuff happening around them. They need to see the important, invisible things. That's because everything has a spirit. People, dogs, pigeons, rocks even. When I go surfing in the ocean, I understand the invisible energy within waves. And waves have spirit, of course. They have hidden energy coils and they have personalities. They are like phone calls from God. They are like faxes from the angels or email from really great dead relatives. Waves are all those things. Surfing allows me to connect with the deep energy patterns of the sea, maybe the planet and, ultimately, the universe. But I see I'm getting carried away and, if I'm not careful, I could become a preachy, verbose tedious kind of shaman, the kind who has to hit you over the head with a bag of hammers, so I'll go slower.

Modern life and technology apparently hamper our ability to make spiritual connections. Nature plugs us back in. One good rock picked up on foggy Lawrencetown Beach at eight in the morning can do that. I might be walking my dog who has again given herself license to pee on everything she can get near. I pick up my one rock and decide it is a healing rock. I carry it around and stroke it and talk to it with my silent words and it connects me. Perhaps soon I will take this rock and use it to heal me or someone else in some inexplicable way. That's how it could work.

Once when I taught history at a private school for rich, messed-up kids, nothing was working. I was trying to teach them about World War I, which I thought was a pretty important subject. I never understood exactly what World War I was about (it wasn't like World War II) but I was convinced it would be better to teach screwed-up wealthy teenagers about World War I rather than, say, ancient Egypt.

Anyway, World War I was going nowhere so I sidled off into what we referred to at the school as "educational alternatives." One of my projects was to take them out into the woods and encourage everyone to find a rock of any size. Then they had to sit and focus on their rock. They had to deliver into their rock all their *negative* energy, all their bad feelings.

They understood this was a whole lot better than the Battle of the Marne. Then they had to carry the rock around with them through the woods and back to the schoolhouse – a remarkable dilapidated mansion where everything was falling apart. Some complained that their rock was too heavy but that was their fault for having selected such large stones. I didn't have to say this out loud; it was self-evident. I told them they couldn't trade their rocks with each other or chuck them in favour of smaller ones. You had to hang onto the rock you had picked.

A thin wisp of a girl who rarely spoke had selected a small flat piece of mica she had found near a dead hemlock stump. One of the broody, heavy-set, dark-haired boys, the son of a man who owned an airline, had picked up a massive lump of granite. So there we were in the early fall forest walking around with our chosen rocks. I had selected one as well – a totally uninteresting piece of shale. Some of my students made fun of my rock, as if shale wasn't special enough for the project. But that was a good sign. It meant they were paying attention. Whenever students make fun of teachers, it means they are at least awake and aware. When people are awake and aware, they learn things (unless it involves explanations about World War I, maybe).

So we walked. Some grumbled. Some said they liked the smell of the rotting leaves. As usual in any educational environment with young people, someone eventually farted and that led someone to make a very Zen joke, a kind of koan, about whether a fart has any smell at all if someone farts in a forest and there is no one there to smell it. I relate all this because this was one of my early shamanistic forays. I'm trying to establish my credentials because I don't think a good shaman can be just aware or plugged in, hip, ecstatic and elevated. He has to do something with his abilities; he has to teach, he has to heal.

I'm beginning to think teaching and healing are the same.

So we finally made it back to the frog pond which had once been a goldfish pond, there beyond the back doors of the dilapidated mansion school. I asked the kids to focus all their negativity one more time on the rock, to pack it all into the rock. Then, one by one, they were to heave their rocks into the pond. The big chunk of granite went first, sending out waves in big perfect circles, scaring the two frogs that were sitting on lily pads. The thin piece of mica floated for several seconds – a lesson in surface tension, I explained. The other pebbles and stones were pitched in. Each one made a different sound when it entered the water and that surprised everyone including me. Then I dropped in my humble piece of shale. And that was what we did instead of World War I.

The broody guy told me he thought the whole exercise "really sucked" but that was his response to everything. Some claimed that they felt better. Some said they had to "think about it."

My little book tells me that we each have to make a choice to unlock our "shaman potential." I've been pretty stingy with my shamanic potential, my inner self says to me on this sad day of the year. My sadness, I should explain, is related simply to both of my daughters going off to school – one to Scotland and one to Wolfville. This leaves me home alone. I'm rattling around the perimeters of loneliness and despair and have toyed with the idea of sky-diving, binge drinking or really good mood altering herbs or, if that didn't work, prescription drugs.

Already, though, I seem to have abandoned pleasurable self-destruction in favour of a healthy dose of shamanism. Nothing to do but follow it or listen to it sing. My greatest disadvantage, I suppose, in developing into a full-fledged shaman is that I don't have any exotic ethnic heritage. I'm hardly ethnic anything. I'm one of those sorry white people brought up on a bland kind of Protestantism that, once rejected, gives me plenty of leeway to adopt a belief system or religion from another culture but I feel long-since cut off from any kind of roots. I'm a white male writer living in Nova Scotia and originally from New Jersey. Born and bred on cars, shopping malls, public schools and ambition. I'm not quite an aging hippie professional with a pony tail but many people think they can read who I am by my unkempt appearance and long equally unkempt hair.

I reckon there's plenty of Celtic blood swirling around in my veins, and coursing through my heart, sending oxygen to my brain cells. There are Gaels and Celts in my ancestry, no doubt, but their heritage was mostly bulldozed by American culture and I've had to work hard to undo as much of that damage as I can. Surfing, music, writing and Nova Scotia have helped immensely and so there is the definition of what kind of shaman I am: the Nova Scotia writer/singer/surfer kind. Indeed, shamans before me were singers, sometimes using their songs to communicate secret knowledge. Nova Scotia Mi'kmaq medicine men and women listened to trees and seas and rocks speak just like me. Polynesian shamans, I am sure, surfed. Maybe some still do. Maybe someday I'll gather around me an international coterie of like-minded shamans. We'll have a kind of convention here on the shores of Nova Scotia with dancing and drums and really bad-tasting fermented beverages that produce visions.

The word "shaman," I have learned, comes from the Tunguso-Manchurian word *saman*, meaning "someone who knows." I know next to nothing about the Tungus people except for the fact that they were nomadic. Some hunted, some fished, and they generally had a reasonably good life of it rambling around the sub-arctic woods of eastern Siberia. None surfed but they had shamans who communed with spirits, wrote spoken word kind of songs and fixed stuff that was broken – especially people. They had plenty of annoying neighbours like Genghis Khan and the Manchurians and they got screwed over by the combined industrial and Russian revolutions and the shamans probably took it pretty badly.

I'm going to be pretty careful about my shamanism so I don't get accused of ripping off any indigenous people. I'm thinking about giving up the small dull pleasure of watching TV as part of my shamanism because I have a hunch that TV cuts you off somehow from what they call the "spiritual essence" of the planet. Television lacks "spiritual essence" for the most part (with the possible exception of *Star Trek* and old *All in the Family* reruns). TV becomes a dismal vice for most of us, but it provides a sharp contrast to the wisdom and sometimes ecstasy of the shamans.

I must now confess that part of my income is derived from the television industry. Hosting a national TV talk show, I am one of those disembodied talking heads who ask supposedly intelligent questions of my guests – all of whom are writers. If the shamanism thing works out and if I can figure out how to wrestle the blandness out of one small corner of the television industry, I may even start a shaman TV show or, better yet, a shaman network. We could have shamanic sports shows, cooking shows and sitcoms like *Shaman in the Family*.

But one small step at a time. I'm convinced that shamanism is a democratic thing, so almost anyone could probably become a shaman. I know I'm not like a black belt shaman; I'm still the gum-chewing kid, goofing-around-at-the-back-of-the-classroom kind of shaman. This is the kind of shaman I am. I think the whole world is sacred and funny at the same time. I'm not big on solemnity. It's even a word that I have trouble pronouncing. I know you have to work at being a shaman, though. You have to practise it just like learning to surf or play the ocarina. I have strengths and I have weaknesses and it may be that my weaknesses will teach me more than my strengths.

In surfing, when a really big wave smacks you off your board and then punches you around, grinds you under in the rage and roil of white-water, it's often better not to fight it. You go limp and save energy, sink and let the energy pass by. If you fight it, you tend to get chundered and chewed. And if the water is cold, it screws around with your attitude towards life. I know that the wave is probably not trying to kill me. It is not seeking revenge. It is its own animate powerful wave-self that is writing this big eloquent opera of energy and transformation. When the wave finally crashes ashore, it is temporarily over. It dies or becomes something else invisible. And I come up sucking sweet, cold air above the sea like a good little surfer shaman should after a wipe out.

"Innate wisdom has to be nurtured," says my guidebook to shamanism. Of course it does. The hard part for an apprentice surf musician shaman like me is figuring out which wisdom is innate. Is it all that stuff I did *not* learn in school, from TV or even from my parents? Some of what I learned from my grandmother, Minnie, may have been innate, though. She always seemed to be more in touch with something larger and more important.

Communing with dogs, birds, leaves and marsh grass is probably working in the innate territory. The problem with most of the innate wisdom is that if you try to pin it down with words, it ends up sounding like a bumper sticker or a sentence out of one of those really bad new age books. So for now, I don't want to say too much about innate wisdom except that it needs nurturing. You plant the tomato seed, make sure it's in good dirt and that it gets rain and sun. Weed around it if you have a lot of weeds where you live. And don't let it watch too much TV.

The experts (at least the one who wrote the little 64 page book I am reading) say that grandmothers and grandfathers are often shamans. This seems to be true in places like Australia and New Zealand anyway – or at least it was before the white people came on ships and began pouring Christianity, like wet concrete, all over the land and the beliefs. But maybe I can assume that both of my grandparents, Minnie and Gaga, were shamans. They farmed the earth after all and they nurtured it. My grandfather kept replenishing the soil with mountains of chicken and cow manure that he believed in like religion. The township was often after him because of the smell but he was a hard-core composter of animal faecal matter well before it became fashionable. In those days, he was threatened with a fine. Today, if he were alive, he'd get some kind of a medal. My grandfather also understood the animate nature of seemingly inanimate things – like the lima bean wire and old International Harvester tractors that either started or not according to their "disposition." My grandfather was innately aware of the dark forces of township politics and automobiles not made by General Motors. But he was also in tune with the succulent life-

ration of Rutgers Big Boy tomatoes and Jersey sweet yellow
c...1.

Minnie's shamanism expressed itself at the piano (the one now in my own Nova Scotian home) where she once sang old warbly songs full tilt. She had powerful advice for me often. When something really rotten happened in my life, like when I would get dumped by a girlfriend or some thieves would steal my car from the Moorestown Mall, she'd say things like, "Just let it go. Stew over it for a while if you have to and then just get on with the next thing." It was probably more the way she said it than the advice itself. But they were healing words. If I still felt bad, she'd give me a fresh uncooked egg and tell me to go throw it at something. I would feel better after that.

Grandparents were surely a little closer to the innate wisdom, especially the ones like mine still connected to the soil through farming. My own parents were one step slightly removed and my brother and I were hopeless products of a 1950s childhood. When I was eight, my current guru (although I didn't use the word then) was Ricky Nelson, who presented his cool, blue-eyed self every week on *Ozzie and Harriet*. He seemed so wise and together and all those girls would scream and holler if he sang "Travelin' Man" in his living room. Although Ricky would eventually die in an airplane crash as the result of freebasing cocaine at 30,000 feet, he was, I think, a good guy laid waste by a childhood of superstardom. Kids should not be allowed to be famous.

It was Ricky Nelson, however, who pointed me towards music, and I started on an old Sears and Roebuck catalogue guitar that was black and had a red-stencilled image of cowboys sitting around the campfire on the front. He also inadvertently taught me how to be relaxed while performing on TV. Ricky always looked like he was about to fall asleep, even when all the girls with knee socks were screaming in his living room and Ozzie pretended to be bopping to "Hello Mary Lou (Goodbye Heart)."

My point seems to be that gurus and shamans are where you find them. I've sullied my argument about TV being bad for the spirit now. I can see that. But my shamanism, I hope, is pretty flexible and non-dogmatic. I'm not locked into any belief system but am cobbling together a patchwork shamanism that involves considerable unlikely and eclectic ideas and activities.

"A crisis may open the door to deeper understanding," says David Lawson in *So You Want to be a Shaman*. The book comes from a press in Berkeley, California, a perfectly logical place for such a book to be published. I would guess that David Lawson is mostly bald with a pony tail and has a really broad, infectious smile. I can see him shopping for fresh vegetables at the farm market in San Francisco by the bay or maybe buying antique furniture in the Castro district of the city. He probably hangs out a lot at City Lights Books. Like the rest of us, he's borrowing heavily on the literature that has come before him. He's a kind of spiritual moonshiner who starts with this big funky mash of fermenting juices and distils it down to essentials. I'm more like a reverse-moonshiner, taking some simple powerful potion and turning it back to funky mash.

I know I have rusty hinges on my door to deeper understanding but I'm not entirely clueless. I stand mute in the middle of a forest and feel awe. I walk around elegant spider webs the size of trash can lids that are strung in my path. I pick up toads sitting in the gravel road waiting to be squashed by truck tires and move them into the weeds. I talk to the west wind like Shelley. I expect clouds to take the form of puffy dragons and breathe truth into the world.

According to notions of "shamanic death" we awaken during moments of upheaval or crisis. Sometimes it is not a complete tragedy, just a nervous breakdown or depression.

I've been palling around with depression for about two years. Fortunately, I have strong inner voices urging me away from nervous breakdowns and extended despair. I keep depression on a short leash. This morning I was depressed, genuinely so, but instead of unpacking the road map to clinical depression or the self-help kit to a nervous breakdown, I decided to become a shaman instead. The world may or may not thank me for this.

Not too long ago, I was involved in saving a kayaker who had been swamped by hurricane-generated waves. I saw him from the headland, paddled out, and successfully got him to shore. It's odd to say this, but I was pretty certain that going out to sea and saving the swamped kayaker would fix me up into a new person. Getting punished by waves that tried to drown me on that occasion, and doing my good deed and making it safely back to shore – I really thought that would shine me up like vinegar on an old penny. But the good stuff is like the bad stuff, I guess. It comes and it goes. Once I dried myself off, I was still the same old sad me. So I'm back to Minnie's advice: "Stew over it for a while and then let it go. Get on to the next thing."

"The next thing" is the rebirth element. The sea rescue was a good little ritual, and the depression I felt was a fairly successful "dark night of the soul." There was a lot of other junk I've been involved in that probably provided me a good foundation for sloughing off fears and negative expectations. I don't necessarily believe that "everything happens for a purpose." Neither of my grandparents or my parents ever said that to me. But I do think that if we weren't so enamoured with the idea that time is linear and that it only moves foreword – like some kind of old Buick with a defective gearbox that has no reverse – I think we would make better sense of how events in the past link up to the present. And if we could diminish the great god Chronos to speak only in hushed whispers, if we could invade the present and occupy that country more often, then we'd probably see that the meaning is in the process – in the doing, in the now.

So I vow to spend more time communing with spirits. This is partly an internal thing, for sure: voices of my grandparents, now dead, great voices in literature, fragments of inspiration silting over in the back of my brain, buried under clutter. It's probably an external thing too. Spirit need not have physical geography but as a physical being, I need to spend time in great physical places. The sea, of course. The shore. Hiking to tops of drumlins, sitting on mossy stones by creek beds, or watching skater bugs on the surface of the water.

I'm hoping, of course, that my newfound shamanism will truly make me a happier person. Yet we all have sadness to lug around. I will learn from it but will not let it dominate me. Sadness and longing are signatures of my tribe. They are tattooed on my heart but through that heart races my red Celtic blood filled with the oxygen granted me freely by the air that envelopes this small blue-green planet, a planet that is ruled by endless celebrations. And, lucky for me, I've been invited to so many of those festive occasions that I've lost count.

July 15

Raising the Teenage Blue Jay

It's July 15th and I'm trying to write in my office, which is filled with the squalling of a teenage blue jay. He's the latest guest in our house, brought here by Sunyata from the wildlife refuge. He is just starting to get his adult squawk – a great shrieking noise that will serve him well once he is released into the wild.

It was a fine blue surfing morning with a head-high peak at a place we call "the Reef," so I have had a full face of sun and some great moments of euphoria. Now it's just me and the blue jay and this attempt to write.

The blue jay has been with us for more than a week and he gets shuttled from one place to another in the house since he is so noisy. Sometimes he wakes up the family too early by pecking hard at the metal bars of his cage, creating something that reminds me of experimental music I once heard in a coffee house in Greenwich Village. He is growing up quickly but still likes to be fed by hand. You pinch some canned cat food into your fingers and then he opens his mouth ever so wide – this is still the baby jay in him – and then you drop it right down his throat. He makes a kind of gurgling noise of satisfaction that lets you know you've done your job well.

This morning I've freed him from his cage and I decide to let him roam around my office. He's just learning to fly and does the obligatory bird-inside-the-house crash into the window. Undaunted, he settles on the sill and ruffles his feathers as I toss him a crumb of my toast which he studies, then consumes, afterwards popping up the crown of feathers on his head which seems to say that he is much pleased with himself and the world as it is.

He flies around my office some more, landing on a copy of *The Anatomy of Melancholy*, then *Finnegan's Wake*, then flying to sit on my electric guitar case, reminding me that I have not played much guitar lately and the guitar itself, bought in 1965 at the Eighth Street Music Store in Philadelphia, is begrudging me the fact that I have not written any songs for it lately. Next the blue jay flies to sit on a cardboard box filled with 35 mm slides. He pulls at the tape and pecks at the cardboard and then drops down to sit on software for learning the Japanese language. He pecks at photographs of cherry blossoms on the cover.

Last night I was reading an F. Scott Fitzgerald story and wondering why so many of that author's characters spent a considerable amount of time and energy bemoaning the fact they were not as rich as the next person. I sometimes assign myself the role of critic of famous writers and this morning as I waded out in the clear blue Atlantic I had a silent dialogue with F. Scott Fitzgerald, telling him he should have been getting on with deeper concerns.

Why I wanted to be surfing with F. Scott Fitzgerald is not clear to me and I should have left him on shore, but he and Gatsby and the characters in that story paddled out with me and we punched through a good clean set of overhead walls of water. I told the author that I really liked his novel, *Tender is the Night*. Now there was a really sad, depressing but beautiful book that I admired because it was full of heartbreak and loss and self-pity but love was at the heart of it and, for God's sake, love has to be more worthy to write about than ambition.

The blue jay has remained unnamed for some reason up to now but, as I write this, I begin a fishing expedition for a good name. Wasn't the Great Gatsby's first name Jay? Or should I just name him after Gatsby's author, F. Scott Fitzgerald? The bird is currently sitting on my bookcase, aggressively pecking at Anaïs Nin's *Cities of the Interior*, one of those books I intended to read but never will. Then he preens himself and, with great aplomb, defecates on Tom Wolfe's *The Purple Decade* – now truly purpled by the orphaned bird.

A blue jay at this age is a curious creature when given free rein of my office and he is partially using the opportunity to learn to fly better once he is released into the great outdoors. Soon, he will be free and on his own, although I hope he stays around so I can feed him by hand once in a while and he can remain my friend. I'm still under the impression that I need all the friends I can muster in this life. I see that he's found his reflection in the stainless steel chimney pipe of my woodstove. He fluffs up his feathers again, galvanized by his own likeness, but gets distracted by a dead fly he spies on the windowsill and hops there to eat it. Next, he begins pecking at random things, testing them to see if they are edible.

Of course, testing the world is what a teenager does best. I remember testing my own teenage strength. Testing my courage – decided I had lots but the teenage years were not the ones to waste it on. Testing my intelligence – smarter than some, though not as smart as the best. Testing my emotions. When I decided that I was fully in love with a girl, I went over the top and soon learned this was not a good teenage guy thing to do. I would fall hopelessly and unrequitedly in love with the object of my desire – a girl who I did not even have the courage to talk to. I became a whimpering F. Scott Fitzgerald kind of teenager. It was the wrong decade for that so I soon gave it up, but probably not soon enough.

Now the blue jay is sitting on my shoulder and watching me peck at the keyboard, wondering what I am all about. He is happy here, squawking in my ear and pecking at my hair but will not be satisfied so he flies back to *Finnegan's Wake*, then on to land on a giant polypore that Sunyata once gave me for a birthday present. In case you don't know, a polypore is a hard giant fungus that grows on the side of trees. It looks like the saucer section of the Starship *Enterprise* and is edible, I think, but a little tough. This is a grand old polypore, two feet across. Sunyata bought it for a dollar at a yard sale. The woman's husband, now dead, had once owned it and she never ever understood why her husband wanted to keep a polypore. But I certainly understood and now it's mine.

The blue jay finds a small pebble on my desk and plays with it for a time until he mistakenly decides it is edible and swallows it. I yell at him from across the room but the blue jay pays no attention. It is fully swallowed but he pops it back up his throat and cradles it in his beak, gazing again around the world of my office with a look on his face that suggests he believes himself to be very clever. I tell him to put the pebble down, that it is an important pebble that I have brought home from western Ireland. I carried the pebble down from Craigh Patrick, the mountain from which St. Patrick banished all the snakes from Ireland. He did such a damn fine job of it that if you even tried to bring a snake to Ireland, rowing over in a boat from Wales perhaps, it would die before reaching the shores of the Emerald Isle.

I still fear the blue jay might choke but he seems to have his own opinion about what he can or can't put in his mouth. So this pebble prompts me to come up with a suitable name for the bird, at least a temporary one. I'll be damned if I'll name him after F. Scott Fitzgerald, the American writer who was the supposed spokesman of his Jazz Age generation. I can't name a bird after him, even though he did such a good job with *Tender is the Night*.

Instead, I'll name the bird Demosthenes. This famous, but now out of fashion, orator and statesmen lived 384 to 322 BC. (Remember the numbers go backwards if you were lucky enough to live in the BC years.) Demosthenes wrote about politics and oratory and he was a famous speechmaker, delivering speeches to old Greeks about what they should or shouldn't be doing. He was famous for his opinions and, looking back, we know that some of his opinions were bang on and others not. This can also be said of the blue jay. He is of the opinion that a dead fly is edible – which is correct in his instance – but he is also of the opinion that the eraser on my pencil or a paper clip has nutritional value, and of course he is wrong. But there is a more compelling reason to name the bird Demosthenes. Despite his passion for oratory, Demosthenes could not pronounce the letter "P." I don't know much Greek but it seems that "P" would be a rather important letter of the alphabet. Just imagine a great politician today trying to give a speech without being able to use the letter "P." He couldn't use words like "politics" or "people," "popular" or "important" or even "proper" and, well, the list goes on. You'd have to hire a terribly clever speech writer to write your speeches so you could do the whole thing without having to use the letter "P." Or maybe you'd just have to get on with it, anyway. "We are roud to be here among such fine eople gathering before arliament today in this great land of lenty. We take ride in our ability to reresent you and romote the health and well-being of all." But if addressing Catholics it would probably be unwise to refer to their leader as the "ope."

Demosthenes was determined to overcome his speech defect and his technique was twofold. His first method was to run a goodly distance until he was out of breath and then recite memorized poetry as rapidly as he could. Why this would work is beyond most of us, but Demosthenes was determined. His second method, and the reason I have named the blue jay after him, is because the Greek orator would try to overcome his problem with the letter "P" by speaking with pebbles in his mouth. How many pebbles or what kind of rocks they were are not known by modern scholars but apparently it helped.

In my early days of writing, I wrote short stories on the old Smith Corona without the letter "G." I would always have to go in and pencil in the "G" by hand afterwards, trying to make it look like a real typewritten letter. I was not very good at it and eventually tried soldering the fallen "G" back on with a soldering gun. The results from that attempt were not good either. But like Demosthenes with the pebbles in his mouth, I did not simply stop writing because I had no "G" on my typewriter. And I refused to try to write short stories without the letter "G" in the words. So I made the best of it.

Demosthenes gave speeches trying to warn the people of Athens that Philip II of Macedonia wanted to invade and conquer them. At first, he was laughed at (it could have been the "P" problem) but eventually his kinsmen awakened to the worry. Some time later Demosthenes got himself in trouble. He was charged with financial corruption, cowardice in battle and, worst of all, indecisiveness in policy making.

Of the three, I would say that a certain amount of indecision and a fair display of cowardice in battle are not so bad. One leads to avoiding truly bad decisions made by hotheads who articulate well while making snap judgements on things they don't understand. Cowardice in battle means you live on as a coward instead of dying as a hero. If there were only enough cowards on any battlefield, the war would end and peace would ensue. But try explaining these things to your Athenian neighbours.

Fortunately for Demosthenes, he gave truly great speeches – finally without pebbles in his mouth – and he was vindicated. He explained away the charges of corruption, cowardice and indecision and he became well-liked and famous for his oratory.

F. Scott Fitzgerald, on the other hand, ended up in Hollywood writing screenplays, which is not nearly as honourable, so I will not name the blue jay after him.

When the day comes that I release my teenage blue jay out into the bright open world beyond the back door, I am hoping he remembers everything he learned, everything I taught him this day while writing in my office. Like Demosthenes freeing himself of the accusations in his famous speech, my friend, the blue-winged, ever-curious Demosthenes, will fly freely into the heavens. Perhaps he will circle my house and keep a keen eye on me, the writer, as I sit at my computer by the big picture window believing that writing will provide the means to free myself of the psychological defects that limit me and keep me earthbound.

July 19

Fathomless and Bottomless

My grandfather told me that in the American South, they shake hands sideways – side-to-side. It's not really a shake but a sway, a kind of dance. It's worth trying when you go to shake hands with someone you don't know. Don't go up and down but move gently side to side.

So far today there was a small argument about time at the breakfast table. Time seems to be a constant source of debate and opinion. My search for timelessness – being perfectly inside of the moment – often seems futile. All too often I am moving into the future before I've had my fair shake at being in the present.

But I'm not good at keeping track of the future, either. The future for me needs to be written down somewhere. Let's say I have to go to such and such a school on the eighteenth to talk about creativity. If I've written it down, I am reminded of this and I get there on time. If not, then no writer arrives for the kids and no creativity lecture. Whatever I write down happens. What I don't write down will be forgotten. This is sadly true of the present and the past as well as the future so I need to remind myself to write it all down, the scheduled and the unscheduled events and notions that make up my life.

Like Sunyata's friend, Becky Jeppeson, knocking at my door at eight in the morning. She found an injured porcupine on the road by the beach and was wondering if I had leather gloves and a box. She wanted to pick it up and drive it to a vet in Dartmouth. It was a foggy morning for sure and the porcupine probably was taking his time crossing the road. Becky did not hit the porcupine but somebody else did. I offered to help her and said I'd meet her there by the injured creature. So I found gloves and a big box, apologized to my dog for not taking her for a walk, had one small final argument about time with myself, gathered some old blue jeans and a shovel to help pick up the porcupine and drove around in the fog until I found Becky standing by the side of the road alongside an unmoving porcupine.

I arrived just after the porcupine died. "He kicked," was the way Becky put it. I'm pretty sure I saw the last spasm of life leaving the porcupine as I eased to a stop in the fog. I leaned close to see if the porcupine was breathing, which was probably not a great idea but, as it turned out, the porcupine had indeed "kicked," which made us both feel sadder than we had been ten minutes ago. And so that was the beginning of my day.

I wandered on the beach along a thin ribbon of sand with the sea on one side, an audience of a million rocks on the other and the fog above, reminding me that if I was going to continue to claim to be a writer, I better damn well do some writing.

I went home and procrastinated as I poured myself some tea and then I read a little of John Irving's *A Widow for One Year*. The phone rang, telling me I had printing work to pick up at a place called Etcetera Print. And then I sat down at my Compaq 286 with its old semi-reliable monochrome screen that shakes up and down a little bit because it is so old. I think of it as slightly palsied and sometimes the Compaq's memory gets filled up and it says it can't hold any more of anything I write. It seems to be telling me, "I can't take it anymore," but it is too polite for that. It means that in order for me to put anything more into it, I need to download and then delete something already stored. It is not at all different from me in that regard.

This year I had stuffed my brain with too much of everything and have tried to free up a little space on my hard drive. Writing things down will allow me to do that. I can fix something solidly into print and then move on to think about newer things if there is enough time.

Sitting beside my desk today are two books: Norman Vincent Peale's *The Tough-Minded Optimist* and *The Politics of Experience* by R.D. Laing. Norman Vincent Peale sums up things at the end of chapters because he's such a no-nonsense kind of guy. He's a bit too religious for me but I've always liked his good-natured, naive optimism. Toward the end of an early chapter he says this: "Become a possibilitarian. No matter how dark things seem to be or actually are, raise your sights and see the possibilities – *always* see them, for they are always there." I like the phrase "or actually are."

I too want to become a possibilitarian. I already am in many ways, I think, or was before I encountered my own recent version of "No matter how dark things seem to be or actually are." There was a good deal of actuality to my darkness but I've been trying to hammer my way out of the bag and I haven't given up. Heeding Mr. Peale's advice and advancing the cause, maybe I should start an organization or political party called the Possibilitarians, although seven syllables is likely to scare off people. We could have our own secret handshake that suggests all things are possible – or most things anyway.

There was nothing I could do this morning to bring the porcupine back to life. He looked like he had been a very healthy porcupine up until the time he was run over. Sometimes porcupines look ratty and not well fed. This one had probably feasted on one of my neighbour's apple trees. When not eating green apples, they feast on twigs and strip the bark from such trees, sometimes killing them. Once I had to capture a porcupine that was destroying my apple tree in the middle of the day. I gently nudged him with a rake into a plastic garbage can to drive him away. I did this while a visitor from West Africa was watching. He was a German man, actually, who was living in the second poorest country in the world because he preferred it to Germany. He preferred Africa because, he said, Africans were not obsessed with being on time. The Germans did everything according to schedules and the Africans he knew had no schedules. Most of them had no computers, no cell phones, no watches and not even pens to write down schedules. They were without time obligations. The German thought my humane capture of the porcupine was what Canadians did for fun.

I, of course, could not harm the porcupine but, instead, drove him away and let him go. Then I wrote a story about it. I write everything down in a notebook and when my pen runs out of ink, I shake it three or four times like an old thermometer until it allows me to put a few more words down on the page.

Now, the other book on my desk on this day is *The Politics of Experience* by R.D. Laing. The cover is dusty because it is a book I've had since college. R.D. Laing was a kind of radical psychiatrist, in case you don't remember him. He said basically that it's completely okay to be crazy. What is normal, after all? He points out that normal men have killed a hundred million people in the last fifty years. The book came out in 1967 and many more have been killed by such normality since. Notice that neither R.D. nor myself would put quotation marks around the word normal. Laing didn't call them "so-called normal." He just called them normal.

I was only nineteen when I read the book first and I already knew I never wanted to be normal. Normal sucked. Almost everything that was normal I was opposed to. Normal meant ordinary. And that equalled dull.

Laing asserts that the condition of "being out of one's mind" is the condition of being normal. And society "highly values the normal man."

Laing doesn't have that upbeat flair for making sullen people cheerful like Norman Vincent Peale does. He is sullen but notes that allowing people to be "original" and unique is good even if society labels them schizophrenic or nuts. Laing worries about alienation. To be alienated from the normal society with all those dull and normal people is healthy in his view. I do still feel a certain alienation from other people (something I've been carrying around since a teenager) but it's not one of the great "dark things" in my life.

Most of my darkness is self-imposed and childish. I sometimes cradle my disappointments. Good friends disappoint me or I disappoint myself. Then I spiral back down into a deep, cold well, although it's not inky black like squid ink there. It's just rather cold and murky. I've been trying to climb up out of the well and lock a lid down tight on it for two years now but I keep finding my way back down there. I regret that I'm not as naive as I used to be. When I was naive I was happier.

My grandfather, known to his grandchildren as Gaga, was happiest when he was selling corn to his neighbours. He grew the corn – at least he planted it. I weeded and suckered the plants (don't get me going on suckering) but he usually picked the ears of ripe, full-bodied sweet corn. He sold the corn for something like 90 cents a dozen. People would drive up the long driveway and my grandfather would shake the hand of the person who was his neighbour and then go out into the field and cut the corn. Talk about fresh.

My grandfather did not grow white corn. He hated white corn almost as much as he hated Harry Truman or a snarled roll of lima bean wire. Gaga only believed in yellow corn and that's what he sold. He called white corn "horse corn" and let people know that he thought only fools would buy horse corn to feed their families but then people who bought corn from a supermarket, corn that came from out of state, didn't know anything about corn, anyway.

My grandfather knew all about growing corn in the hot South Jersey summers. In August, he walked around with a machete just in case anyone drove up to buy corn. He was always ready with a sharp machete to cut yellow corn in the sweltering summer heat. But I don't think the corn made him as happy as just talking to the people who drove up. "Jawing," my grandmother Minnie called it. He would jaw with whoever it was. He was a great talker, Gaga was. He could talk the face off a mule. He had opinions about everything but only expressed his darkest opinions to me. He'd explain who was to blame for the Great Depression, or how Harry Truman couldn't run his own business so he went into politics and became president of the United States. "The man couldn't run a hardware store but he was in the White House," is the way Gaga would put it.

I knew from high school history class that it was Truman who had given the go-ahead to drop two atom bombs on Japan, one after the other, but that didn't bother my grandfather nearly as much as the fact that Truman was a Democrat. And my grandfather didn't believe Democrats had any brains at all.

Even when he was ninety years old, with a shaky voice and a shaky hand, Gaga talked about his successful corn crops and aired his uncomplimentary opinions about Democrats. He died a staunch Republican and an everlasting believer in yellow corn.

This is sad to report but I think my grandfather was opposed to optimism. He *expected* things to go wrong. And they did. He would have scoffed at Norman Vincent Peale had the Reverend Peale pulled up one hot August day to buy yellow corn and, while shooting the breeze with Gaga, accidentally used a phrase like "tough-minded optimism." The two of them would have probably jawed for awhile until the heat got to them because they were both talkers but Peale would not understand my grandfather's pessimism that the pheasants and racoons were trying to ruin him, the porcupines were trying to steal his profits, and the black smut disease was trying to rot his precious corn. Peale would have had a hard time trying to make my grandfather see the positive side of these things.

Inside my R.D. Laing book, I discovered a parking pass from CBC TV dated 03/21. No year is noted but March 21st is my birthday. So I was there on my birthday, although it must have been almost ten years ago. Along with the pass is a folded piece of paper titled "Time Capsule." The evidence suggested that I was once asked to appear on a national TV show to tell the audience what I would put in a time capsule. From the looks of it, I had come up with a list of ten things.

1. personal letter. Dear somebody
2. copy of a Maud Lewis painting
3. condom
4. photograph of my beach
5. #2 pencil
6. a book
7. organ donor card
8. cigarette butt or an ashtray
9. an exercise I do with my students: a list of one smell, taste, sound, sight, touch
10. seeds of an endangered species

I had clever explanations written down explaining my selection for each of these. I'm sure that when I was on camera I was nervous and trying to suppress the fact that I was shaking. I shake sometimes when I'm TV nervous. But I knew how to appear to be very relaxed. My notes about the condom reminded me to say this: as a reminder that love and sex both require caring and caution and you should check the expiry date.

Since I can't remember this actual event, it's almost like some other person was on television that day. I wonder if he came off wise and clever as he seems to me now or if the audience thought he was an asshole.

I have a funny feeling I had been reading the R.D. Laing book while warming up, waiting to go on TV. Imagine trying to relax yourself while reading such lines as, "We are afraid to approach the fathomless and bottomless groundlessness of everything." Good thing I didn't say that on TV right after the Ivory liquid commercial.

When my daughters were young, they liked to shake the crab apple tree and make the apples fall from the branches. Sometimes one would shake and one would stand under the tree and laugh while the small, hard apples rained down on her. I would yell at my kids because I believed the apples should be able to stay on the tree until they were ripe and then fall to the ground on their own. I was also afraid that apples falling en masse on my youngest daughter, Pamela, might injure her in some way.

So they shook the apples down mostly when I wasn't around to watch. And at night, while we all slept, the pheasants, deer and porcupines would gather beneath the tree and feast on the fallen fruit. Morning would bring fog or sun and I might notice the chewed apples on the ground. Then I would walk to the beach, smell the salty sea, pop a sour wild cranberry into my mouth and make it explode with my teeth. The song of gulls would fill the air and I would watch waves breaking like folding glass as I sat down and dug my fingers into the cold wet sand. In the sand, I knew, were the hidden secrets to making time stand still but looking back from this vantage point of time, it seems I must have decided to leave them buried there, as my daughters are mostly grown and I am still racing into the unscheduled future.

July 21

The Wings of Morning

My goal today is to again let the blue jay fly freely around my office while I write and I will use his path and the objects he lands upon to guide my writing. This is an ancient Chinese technique to inspire profound wisdom and inspiration, first practiced by the twelfth-century sage Chiu Yiu. Most scholars have ignored Chi Yiu because he fell out of favour down through the centuries but here in East Lawrencetown, he is not forgotten.

I fed Demosthenes first because I thought it unfair to have him working on an empty stomach. He ate his cat food well as I put it on the tip of my finger and he jammed his beak over it so that my finger went well down his throat. Then I treated him to some cooked peas and corn, fed one item at a time until he relented with his "begging." Begging, as historians realize, was once an honourable profession, but it has since fallen out of favour, like rhymed poetry. However, begging works well for Demosthenes, although I must teach better survival skills before he leaves this sanctuary to live on his own in the wilderness. I need to teach him about catching flies and mosquitoes for starters, since blue jays usually feast on such things. Unfortunately, I usually catch flies in my office by smacking them hard with a fly swatter until they fall to the ground. Demosthenes will probably not be much good at using a fly swatter in the wilderness so I'll have to come up with an alternative plan.

So begins the blue jay's path. After his breakfast and release in my office, Demosthenes first flew to Newfoundland, perching precariously on the top of a giant mounted wall map on the north wall of my office. My guess is that since this is his first choice of a perch, it indicates that province will see great wealth and spiritual renewal in the next year. Next, he flew to sit on my electric piano, which has sat unused for these many months. Thus Demosthenes is reminding me that I've been ignoring music for far too long. Good point. Later I will turn the keyboard on and place various bits of food – seeds, cat food, other treats – on the keys themselves and see if I can get Demosthenes to play a tune. Birds are musical by nature, although Demo, along with many of his other blue jay cronies I've met, tends to be a bit on the shrill side. He likes to hop onto things that are unstable like a stack of cassettes or a notice from Revenue Canada on the corner of the desk. Or a pile of pencils fallen over like pick-up sticks. He knocks things over and then looks surprised or perhaps proud of his mischievous deeds. I chase him off the famous polypore because he would like to drill it with his beak. Already he is an accomplished pecking bird, much like the baby woodpecker that he used to bunk with at the wildlife rehab centre.

He is having a grand time inspecting my chaotic, cluttered office. It's as if it were designed exclusively for him, a veritable Blue Jay Disneyworld. One of his favoured places seems to be a slanting drawing table with a top of shiny Formica; he lands near the top and lets gravity skate him towards the bottom and he does this over and over, sliding down the slope as if he were blue jay skiing. When not skiing, he likes nestling in an old robe – actually my grandfather's old blue "housecoat," a blue flannel thing that looks as good as new. Maybe it's the fact that it is blue that makes it so appealing to him.

Knocking over my fluorescent desk lamp, Demosthenes seeks out a higher perch. Chiu Yiu would say that this is to remind us to always seek the higher ground for a better vantage point of what is going on around us so we may avoid danger. If you can put yourself high enough up on a mountain or even in the sky and look down, then everything appears beautiful and orderly. Even Buffalo, New York from 30,000 feet looks pretty. The Rocky Mountains look like they were planned – created by an artist. And human differences "from a distance" as Bette Midler would sing in that song, disappear. This is what Demosthenes is going on about on this brisk, serene morning. I look out my window off to sea and there is an enormous cruise ship waiting to come into Halifax Harbour. These behemoths seem to arrive at night, anchoring off the coast and then entering the harbour in the morning. It has just begun to move and soon it will be docked at Pier 22, disgorging Americans who will spend considerable sums of money in that fair town. As the British poet Arthur Hugh Clough once said, "How pleasant it is to have money," but personally I am with Jean Louis Rudolph Agassiz who, when asked to give a talk for money, said, "I can't waste my time making money."

Demosthenes now knows his name and comes when I call him if I have a smidgen of canned cat food on my forefinger. The only problem here is that when I turn back to my keyboard to write, I smudge the keys with left-over gunk.

The cruise ship is gone now – past the tip of Hartland Point and heading into the harbour. All manner of trades people, swindlers, sellers, pickpockets, tour operators, rickshaw operators, taxi drivers, scarf makers, artists, restaurateurs, ice cream sellers, and coffee vendors are preparing for the arrival of this boatload of Americans aching to lighten their wallets and exercise their credit cards. How different the reception would be if it were a shipload of refugees.

Demosthenes has found my old parking pass from the CBC and he is worrying over it – studying it like it is a sacred text. Chiu

Yiu would understand that this is to remind us that profundity can be found in even the simplest scripts. For example, the parking pass is clearly marked "Temporary," as are all things in this life. It has an effective date (my birthday: 03/21) but no year. This means I could go back to the CBC TV studio and park for free and legitimately each year on my birthday. And this I will do if it turns out I have nothing better to do on those days. I'm not sure why but I'm not fond of birthdays, especially my own. Birthdays seem so traditional and predictable and it means you are another year older. Most people are fond of birthdays but I've always found them to be disappointments. So I may head for the CBC parking lot after all come next March.

Also on the document is an expiration date – again a reminder of one's mortality. The expiration date here is the same day – as if life is one metaphorical day, one brief sun-up to sundown, parked in the CBC parking lot. The number on my CBC parking pass is 2718. When I was 27 it was the year 1978, the year I moved to Canada. When I was 18 the year was 1969, the year I graduated from high school, a grand slam of a year and a summer that was unsurpassed for its roller coaster ride of emotions.

I erratically attended high school dances leading up to that tumultuous summer of 1969 (We never called it the summer of love but looking back it was certainly that in spades.) and the bands often played oldies. The line "See the pyramids along the Nile" sticks out in my head, played live by a group who called themselves The Trojans, after a brand of condom. It was a genius stroke of band naming. I forget why I was supposed to "see those pyramids along the Nile" but it was a slow dance song and if I could muster up the courage to ask Cherie Devlin or Kathy Suga or Kathy Kurtz or Cathy Hafner – so many Cathies back then – I would hold her close and dance poorly but adequately until the song was over. I would believe that Cherie or one of the Cathies was in love with me and we were in Egypt gazing at those sand-worn monuments to dead pharaohs. But soon the song was over and I was back to being lost and lonely, which was my nature as a lad.

It seemed that there were many oldies that globbed onto concepts involving the "Seven Wonders of the World." It kept coming up over and over. Often it was a comparative device, a metaphor or hyperbole suggesting that "you," the girl in the song, were much more interesting than any of the Seven Wonders. None could hold a candle to the girl. Now, thanks to the tip-off by the Trojans, we realized that the pyramids were one of the Seven Wonders of the World. But what were the others? It was actually a bit confusing because there was some debate over the exact selection of the Seven Wonders. In fact, there were at least fourteen wonders because there were seven wonders of the ancient world and seven wonders of the Middle Ages. In high school, my friends and I didn't give a rat's ass about such things but now that I am over fifty and sitting in my office, prompted by Demosthenes to think about these things, I'd like to nail it down once and for all.

So, aside from the pyramids on the big seven ancient list, there were the Hanging Gardens of Babylon built by a guy with the way-cool name of Nebuchadnezzar (a truly suitable moniker for a metal band). There was a statue of Zeus made of ivory. The Colossus of Rhodes came next, another statue 120 feet high, made of bronze. Next was The Temple of Dianna at Ephesus. As I write this, Demosthenes flies about my office and eventually crashes into my fax machine, suggesting that there is something here I should not ignore. Hmm. Dianna was the goddess of hunting and chastity. The two do not seem linked in any obvious way and I am not sure what I would do with this information but the day is not over yet. I'll file it for later pondering.

Number six on the Seven Wonders of the ancient world hit parade is the Mausoleum at Halicarnassus. Now, that never once was mentioned in any of the oldies songs I can remember. And you can see why the lyricist who wrote "You Belong to Me" did not write, "See the Mausoleum at Halicarnassus." But now you know about it and can use it in a lyric that can be part of the soundtrack of your life, if you like. Number seven was the lighthouse at

Alexandria, standing either two hundred feet high or six hundred feet high. Scholars are still arguing about this. It was built during the reign of Ptolemy II who was undoubtedly one heavy dude.

And so the morning progresses and coffee is indicated – "indicated" is a verb I hear doctors use. It is a very weak verb, I think, and replaceable with something more direct: "Take this." "Do this or you might not live long."

I'm worried now, like any good parent, that I'm not preparing Demosthenes in any useful way for his ultimate release. Flying around my office is not the same as flying around outdoors. Today, for example, he has learned that it is not a good idea to fly directly into a fax machine. In the wilderness, there are few fax machines he needs to worry about but, instead, hawks and owls. In the wilderness, too, there will be no tins of cat food for him to find or Green Giant canned corn. To that end I will try to find him more bugs.

My hope is, of course, that he will live up in the tree and come down to me to eat out of my hand for a month or so until his wild nature takes over and he acclimatizes to the outdoors. There is much to worry about. Even now he is sitting on a pile of invoices, flipping the pages up one at a time like a public accountant auditing the books at WorldCom or Xerox. This too will not help him to survive but maybe it is what the job counsellors would call a "transferable skill." I certainly hope so.

Demosthenes worries the pebble on my desk again but does not try to swallow it. The very pebble that helped me name him indicates that he is learning lessons. He preens himself every time I ruffle my own hair. Hair ruffling helps me write better, I find, so Demosthenes fluffs up and tries to get his feathers more orderly each time I need ruffling. He sometimes flies and lands right on my head or my shoulder. When he is not knocking lamps over or investigating encoded CBC parking permits, he sits on the pile of invoices and looks at his reflection again in the stainless steel pipe of my woodstove. Upon his release, he will, one hopes, seek out others of his kind. What will they make of him and his tales of being raised inside my house? Will they believe him when he speaks of giant polypores, invoices, fax machines that will not budge and a writer ruffling his hair as he writes?

I remember what Arthur Koestler once wrote: "One may not regard the world as a sort of metaphysical brothel for emotions." But I have grown fond and attached to the jay. There will be joy and sadness at his parting, for, as Arthur Schopenhauer pointed out, "Every parting gives a foretaste of death."

Schopenhauer also noted, however, that "every coming together again [provides] a foretaste of resurrection." And that is where Chiu Yiu would want me to end my survey of the morning. For, while writing is an act of discovery and an attempt to understand, record and pass on the experiences of living, reading is also an act of resurrection. To write is to live; to read is to give new blue jay wings to every moment of awareness that has come before.

July 24

In Search of Majapahit

My summer research again took me to the garden. My intent was to write a travel story, a chapter, or an entire book, about places I have travelled to. But instead of going around the world, I was returning to my garden where I had once spent a productive morning waiting for insects to arrive so I could write about them. I decided to try this again, insects or not.

I have, of course, travelled far and wide. Sometimes I found things to write about, sometimes not. Portugal is a fine country, for example, but I only found a couple of poems there. Spain was good for three more poems but that was about it. There were no grand themes for me there. I just wasn't looking in the right places.

So it was out the door with a pile of books and a good attitude and across the gravel road into my garden by the marsh. I like to think my garden is a kind of performance piece. I had hauled the seaweed, tilled it in one shovelful at a time, planted some seeds and then waited for the performance to begin. It was the tail end of July now and the show was well under way. The audience returned to see how things were going.

Another bright day, "better than what we deserve," as one of my neighbours would say. I was on my long leash, allowing dalliance without true purpose, travelling as far as my mind would allow me. A Walt Whitman sort of thing, Wordsworthian even – "a man pleased with his own volitions."

"Volition," I admit, is a rather archaic word, not heard much these days. According to the *Oxford English Dictionary*, it means, "A decision or choice made after careful consideration." Or at least it meant that in 1798. My decision, carefully considered – thus, my volition of the moment – was to sit by my garden and continue my journey. And thus was I pleased with it and other decisions NOT to do anything else.

It was a bit warm and muggy and the first creature to present itself for inspection was a deer fly. Frank Lutz's *Field Book on Insects* was with me and now I had a subject to look up. It turns out that the deer fly, the horse fly and the gadfly are all pretty much the same thing. *Tabanus atratus*. It may comfort some to discover, as Lutz states so eloquently, "Only the females bite; the males content themselves with sipping sweets from flowers."

My guess is that there is more to it than that. A contemporary entomologist could probably not get away with that kind of chauvinism, but it wasn't my job this morning to consider anything from a politically correct point of view. I was a stranger in a strange land, a pilgrim with my guides and my guidebooks. Besides, I had always wondered what a true gadfly was. Now I knew, and it seemed appropriate. In literature a gadfly was a tormentor, and horseflies could be just that, but not this one. Mine flew off, a male perhaps, who did not want to bite my flesh, but only to sip "sweets from flowers."

Lutz states that there were 40 different kinds of *Tabanus* and 35 variations of their cousins the *Chrysops*. At least that's how many had been recorded in New Jersey, which must be a famous place for the study of flies, a fact unbeknownst to me who grew up and lived there for over twenty years. "The eyes of the males touch each other above; those of the females somewhat separated." I would take his word on this.

The scribble in my notebook at that moment went like this: "I am in perfect escape from the world – must do this again." The dash suggests this was an aside, as if I was speaking to my future self. It also suggests more pleasure at my own volitions and a secretive nature, as if I had believed I was trying to get away with something forbidden, and succeeding.

It is not a morning for rare or grand bugs. A mosquito arrives and lands on my shirt but does not bite. He looks exactly like the drawn image of the mosquito in the book labelled "*Anopheles*, resting." This one may also be resting or it may be that he too is male.

"Everyone knows a mosquito," says Lutz, "or thinks that he does. The proboscis of the female is fitted for sucking but the male's mouthparts are so rudimentary that he cannot bite." When my daughter was about to leave for Costa Rica for five months, we spent a lot of time worrying about malaria-carrying mosquitoes and which was the right drug to take to prevent infection. One drug, everyone assured us, was inexpensive and worked effectively but made you crazy. The other one was more expensive but it left your sanity intact. There seemed little choice in the matter so we paid the money for the expensive one.

Once she returned from Costa Rica, Sunyata said the drug was a waste of money because she didn't meet a single person with malaria, but a parent errs on the side of safety. I knew mosquitoes were clever and not to be trusted. Even our local Nova Scotia larvae were famous for their ability to stick a tube into aquatic plants to "siphon" air so they did not have to come to the surface to breathe. Now, that was clever, and I'm sure their cousins in Central America had other clever tricks up their sleeves once they had moved beyond the larvae phase. One wanted to be both sane and inoculated in the presence of any mosquitoes who might be carrying malaria.

I had also been at a party once where world travellers were jovially sharing malaria stories. Fevers and hallucinations and near-death experiences seemed to be the norm. I felt sidelined by the animated discussion, never having had malaria or any other potentially fatal tropical disease. All had agreed Africa, Southeast Asia and Brazil were the best places to get malaria and all were convinced that they were somehow glad they had endured the experience. But I wasn't convinced enough to put malarial fever on my agenda. Another good reason to stay close to home and research my next book in my garden.

An osprey shrieked overhead. He was flying back to his nest carrying eelgrass. Sometimes they have a fish, other times it's just eelgrass. My guess is that once an osprey has committed himself to that death-defying dive from twenty feet down through the air and to the bottom of the sea or lake, he feels obliged to grab hold of something. If there is no fish, his talons grab some eelgrass and he flies it home to his nest where there is disappointment all around. "Not eelgrass again," his mate and progeny might whine. In flight, his voice is a "cheep, cheep," which doesn't seem to befit such a noble looking raptor. Peterson also notes that the osprey's call is sometimes "yewk, yewk," although I think the great bird man is lying on that. I have been around ospreys on land and on sea for many years and not a yewk have I heard.

In 1450, the Italian writer Leon Battista Alberti, in his treatise, "The Perfect Country House," set out some guidelines for where to build: "We should carefully avoid bad air and ill soil." He was probably referring to places like New Jersey. It would be hard to build a country home in many parts of New Jersey because there is little "country" left in the Garden State. This is a great tragedy for me, a farm boy from birth who grew up there. So I moved to Nova Scotia where the air was good and the soil was healthy.

Whoever built my old farmhouse a couple of centuries ago even followed Alberti's directive to build "under the shelter of some hill where there is plenty of water, and pleasant prospects." Pleasant prospects. Hmm. This is a good thing, right? Certainly so, despite the fact that a word like "pleasant" is hardly ever heard. The corruption of the English language has caused us to exaggerate so much of everything. A movie is either fantastic or it is terrible. Your vacation was probably wonderful or a disaster. Rarely when asked for an opinion on anything will someone say, "It was pleasant." But my garden, damn it all, is a pleasant place. There are many pleasant aspects here, and today I stopped to smell the wild roses and attune myself to the soil and air, both of fine quality. Alberti would be proud of me.

In the old days, the twelfth and thirteenth century to be slightly more precise, Genghis Khan united the Mongol tribes and my guess is that that had no pleasant aspects. It was a bloody business. By the time Marco Polo had grown restless and trekked off to Asia, Khan's great empire stretched from the Pacific to the Danube and from Siberia south to the Arabian Sea.

Kublai Khan, the subject of Samuel Taylor Coleridge's famous drug-induced poem, inherited this substantial empire and ruled from Peking. He thought it a good idea to keep expanding and had navies attacking Japan and Java, which must have seemed like the right nations to attack at the time. But he met his match and was defeated by the navies of a Hindu-Buddhist kingdom of the sea called Majapahit. After that things started to fall apart for the Khan, due to religious differences and various opinions about boundaries.

My American-Canadian education leaves various holes and gaps when it comes to history. As far as I can tell, Majapahit was never on any quiz or in any history book I read. And I wonder why. Since I know almost nothing about Majapahit, I allow myself to borrow the name and assert to all and none around me that I now dub my several acres of garden and swampland, Majapahit. My navies are an old wobbly canoe buried in the raspberry bushes, and several old surfboards in my Acadian shed. We could be both Hindu and Buddhist if the need arose and should Kublai Khan's navies attack the nearby Elvis Island, just across the water from here on Lawrencetown Lake, we might just paddle over there and kick his butt.

Both Genghis and Kublai Khan, I am sure, were afflicted with what the Buddhists call "The six negative emotions." These were pride, jealousy, desire, ignorance, greed and anger. You'd probably need all six to run an empire stretched across all of Asia and parts of Europe. Coleridge's bucolic "Pleasure dome" was more in his eighteenth century hallucination than in reality. My personal pleasure dome cover, however, is fitted snugly over my head today from horizon to horizon.

On a morning like this, poetic licence in my back pocket, in search of my perfect Majapahit, I admit to being guilty of only two of those Buddhist negative emotions. Pride and desire. I can see how both could get you in trouble but I don't think a body can write without some pride or desire in his or her mental tool kit. So this is probably as pure as I can get although I am told that if I pronounce "Om Mani Padme Hum" enough times, I could rid myself of the last of the negative emotions.

Kublai Khan may have known that the Tibetan word for ego is *dak dzin*, literally meaning "grasping to self," which is not considered a good thing. A Tibetan Buddhist might aspire to be "egoless," a thing very hard to accomplish in the world I live in. We consider people who don't have strong desires and personalities to be uninteresting and unimportant; hence the "couch potato" or maybe we would refer to a person with no strong emotion or actions as a "vegetable."

Few of us aspire to be like my zucchini, peaking out from under the great umbrella leaf of its mother plant, right next to the Mr. Personality Egyptian onion with its tall mast and flag of baby onion clusters atop. Here in Majapahit, the long green squash is the minister of state and the onion the official flag. The garden is the cabinet of advisors and the legislature. The sky is the embassy from which ambassadors arrive, in this case, another sparrow and, at last some colour – an American goldfinch with its "deeply undulating flight." The undulation occurs as the bird rises with a hearty thrust of wings and then pauses, allowing it to fall several inches or more before it flaps again. It rises and falls over and over. What must that feel like? I may never know.

Just for the heck of it, I say, "Om Mani Padme Hum" over and over several times until I fear I may lose track of my ego entirely and give it up. It's as if the sound of my chanting has stirred the insect world, for suddenly there are black flies, mosquitoes and others. I shoo them away with pure thoughts and good intentions and, as usual, it works.

There are swallows now, two of them at least, bringing greetings from other realms as they swoop and swallow the bugs who are now plentiful. They swoop through the airy buffet at high speeds. A bellyful of black flies is happiness to the barn swallow.

In "Self Portrait of a Universal Man," our friend Leon Alberti addresses the qualities desirable for one to be considered "universal." Some of it sounds quaint and occasionally trivial even. The self-portrait suggests he is talking about himself, pleased with his own volitions but not without enemies. He begins as an achiever and an egotist but by midlife, "He despised the pursuit of material gain," and pondered great things "at dinner between courses."

The Universal Man, in his older years, "declared that quadrupeds, birds, and other living things of outstanding beauty were worthy of benevolence," and "when his dog died, he wrote a funeral oration for him," as any good Universal Man should when his mutt moves on.

And, when the world grew too heavy a weight on the Universal Man's shoulders, "The sight of rocks, flowers and especially pleasant places more than once restored him from illness to good health." Like Leon Alberti, I have been torn down, rusted, corroded, even demoted in recent years. Fortunately for me, the bugs, the plants, the birds and the warm sea air have selected me as their restoration project today. Such ambitious compassion amazes me and I sprawl out flat on my back and stare deep into the heavens.

July 27

The Anatomy of Melancholy

My dog Jody had become sick and had not eaten for three days. She was going downhill when I took her to the veterinarian, Julia Weste. There were several visits to her animal clinic and they involved rectal thermometers and blood tests and X-rays. You would have thought something could be discovered but it wasn't.

Now, I promised myself this morning that I would not write about a sick dog, that no one wants to read about a sick and possibly dying dog (because that's what we all feared). People tend to outlive dogs, which may not be such a great thing for the history of the world, but it is a fact we have to live with. And yes, there are these stories we tell others and ourselves about the death and dying of a pet. But I told myself as I awoke this morning I should work on my novel, damn it. I have characters waiting for something to happen in their lives. They are all worried silly that the writer has abandoned them. One is a baffled early-retired history professor from Ottawa. He is in Halifax and he doesn't know why he is there. The main character, Molly – my protagonist, at least I think she is my protagonist – runs a used bookstore on what I call the "forgotten end of Barrington Street." Aside from the young indie band called Dumpster Teeth, the only other significant character is a boy named Todd who is lying in a bed at the IWK Hospital, dying of cancer.

Something interesting is about to happen for Todd before he dies. Eric, the ex-history prof, is about to discover why he is in Halifax but things are about to get very difficult for Molly. And so they wait.

They waited all weekend while I nursed Jody. Jody could not keep anything down. I could go on about dog vomit here, but I realize it is one of those topics that might stop readers dead in their tracks, and then they might retreat to reading gruesome Stephen King novels like *The Shining*. Horror seems much friendlier to read about than dog puke.

But because Jody could not keep anything down, she was losing strength. She was fading quickly until Julia put her on an intravenous drip, which began dripping life-saving saline fluids into the dog's bloodstream. The weekend was coming on and Jody was supposed to go to the emergency animal clinic for a continued IV drip. This clinic is in Burnside Industrial Park. The family did not want their dog living, or dying, in an industrial park. We lobbied for taking Jody home and monitoring the drip.

Julia agreed, although it was probably not one of those things vets are supposed to do. The process involved syringes, needles, a couple of injections to stave off vomiting. It was more complicated than I thought and downright hairy but Sunyata and I undertook the task.

The IV bag hung from the living room book shelves, the long clear plastic line with the life-giving fluids snaking down the shelves past Kerouac's *On the Road*, Salinger's *The Catcher in the Rye*, Carl Jung's *Man and His Symbols* and *The Canadian Writers' Market*. Whenever the dog moved the wrong way, the drip stopped. It needed lots of human attention and Sunyata and I attended to Jody through the night, once having to remove the syringe, inject the catheter line with fluid and reinsert the needle. Tough going at four in the morning.

There was no improvement; Jody continued to vomit what little fluid was in her stomach. But she levelled off. She did not get worse.

I should not tell you this but I positioned a picture of the Pope – the 264th one apparently – by Jody's cage. It is a large colour, glossy photo that fell out of the newspaper because the Pope was in Canada. In the photograph he looks quite old because he is quite old. He is smiling – at least I think it is a smile – and he is waving. Or maybe he was just caught like that with his hand in the air, about to swat a gnat, but I assume he is waving because that is what a Pope does. He waves at crowds. I positioned him and his smile by Jody's face so that he appears to be waving at Jody through her long dark nights. Jody is mostly blind. She's thirteen years old and has cataracts. She's never had any interest in photographs and even gave up interest in TV dogs unless they are barking, in which case she will bark.

But Pope John Paul II was stationed there waving at her just in case.

I am not Catholic and have certain grudges against that church because I've read a lot of history. History reading makes me sober and cynical, a twinning that is never good for one's soul. History also leads me to believe in equations involving what I call harm and good. My mother's view about things like fluorinated water or mosquito control is that they may "do more harm than good." That has often been my feeling about churches, although I wish it were otherwise. Nonetheless, religion brings comfort and that's what I wanted for Jody, so the Pope was involved, God bless him.

In Sir Robert Burton's *The Anatomy of Melancholy*, a book I continually find fascinating, he notes that ancient alchemists concocted something called *aurum potable* – potable gold, gold you could drink. It cured you of all manner of things. "Sometimes it was a rich cordial with pieces of gold leaf floating in it." Like so much of modern medicine, potable gold would be expensive and impressive by its very dearness. The price of the cordial would vary these days and you might have to check the business section of the papers to see whether gold was up or down, whether your *aurum potable* today cost a hundred or two hundred dollars.

I tend to be in favour of all cures if they work, whether they be scientifically provable or not. I gave a friend who has lung cancer a small stone I carried down from Craigh Patrick in Ireland (St. Patrick's Mountain) and he carries it around with him for curative purposes. All he figures is "it can't hurt," and it might work. If I were feeling ambitious today I would call up some business people I know and see if any of them would like to help me resurrect potable gold and sell it like Pepsi on the open market. We'd have to include some tiny amounts of gold in each drink and it would be expensive, but I could see this being something people could believe in. We would make no promises but offer hope. That's always a marketable commodity.

Marketing hope is okay in my moral universe as long as you don't do "more harm than good," so it would have to be marketed carefully. Here's a small toast to *aurum potable*.

Had I lived in a previous century, I would have liked to have been an alchemist, fusing together great, bold concoctions of spiritual beliefs, science, philosophy and hogwash. Burton suggests that the alchemists used *aurum potable* and occasionally other concoctions involving "plants, metals, animals" to cure the likes of "Leprosy, Gout, Dropsy, Falling Sickness, Ulcers, Itches, Furfures, Scabs, Stones, Colic, Palsy, Vertigo, Cramps, Convulsions and Apoplexy." They may not have always worked, but the alchemists and their descendants provided hope for cures in a dark and seemingly indifferent universe.

On this particular Monday morning, Jody is greatly improved. She has survived the weekend. There were car crashes across America, fighter jets smashing into crowds of men, women and children at an air show in the Ukraine (78 dead) and more dead in Palestine. Morgues are brimming with bodies dead from cancer around the world and worse things are happening in poverty-stricken countries that have fallen off our radar.

But Jody is hanging in there. She is drinking freely – a concoction of Campbell's chicken broth, white sugar and well water. This is her *aurum potable*, I believe. Since I cannot get her to eat any solid food yet, I rub her teeth with small pearls of pure honey. She licks her teeth and the honey finds its way into her digestive tract. Dr. Weste suggested using corn syrup, which I didn't have. I almost used molasses but decided honey was the ticket.

So as of this writing, I am optimistic. Maybe you can cure anything with an IV drip, some sugar, chicken broth and well water and, above all, a little honey smeared on the lips and teeth of someone or something you love.

The media reported today that the Pope apologized for the past sins of priests, praised the good ones and encouraged young people to defend the Catholic Church. He smiles and waves, smiles and waves. Elsewhere, nine miners are rescued from a flooded mine in Somerset, Pennsylvania. Canadian troops are back from Afghanistan and Canada is sending the ships HMCS *Summerside* and *Goose Bay* north to "show the flag" in the Arctic as an assertion of sovereignty.

I learned this morning that Winston Churchill directed some of his brightest military experts to set up a program to train English coastal seagulls to spot the periscopes of German subs and then shit on them. Although my research on this subject is incomplete, as is all my research except for the first-hand type, I believe this was a grand plan and would hope all wars could be fought this way. Whichever country can train its seagulls to strategically dollop the most seagull crap on the warships of its enemy should win whatever the conflict. It beats the bejesus out of full-scale nuclear war.

I also read that dogs have played significant roles as "man's best friend." As we all know, not all dogs are friendly. I was attacked once by a Doberman and remember with great clarity the effect of those sharp teeth as they bit into my thigh, the beast having missed my particulars by mere inches. However, once I met the brute's master, I realized that I much preferred the Doberman to the man. He was of the opinion the dog was acting in self-defence even though I had been walking down the road wielding nothing more deadly than the paperback version of *Paradise Lost* I was supposed to be reading for graduate school. I didn't want to read all of *Paradise Lost* but figured if I walked around town long enough with the book in my hand, some of it would sink in by osmosis. Later, as a young professor, I would learn that many of my university students saw their own education in the same fashion.

Dogs, while mostly noble, don't always have great judgement. Like their human counterparts, they have no way of foretelling a bad result from a good deed. A Newfoundland dog, for example, once saved Napoleon Bonaparte from drowning in the sea. This was a bit of irony since Napoleon had always had a distaste for dogs. Laden with a heavy ceremonial sword, Napoleon had fallen off a boat and was sinking. Imagine that he could devise strategies to conquer Europe but not bother to learn the basics of the crawl or the backstroke.

The Newfoundland dog saw Napoleon drowning, dove in and saved the creep. Napoleon had already ravaged much of Europe and he was escaping from the island of Elba where he was in exile. Unfortunately for much of Europe, the Newfoundland dog had not been reading the papers. He was acting on his goodwill instinct when he jumped into the waters to save Napoleon, who was changing boats in his escape. That stupid, heavy sword had put him off balance and sent him into the drink. Apparently, no one involved in his escape could swim. No Frenchmen were diving in to save the bastard but the dog did.

Napoleon, dripping from the chill March swim, continued to dislike dogs despite his salvation by one. He re-established his power base and ruled for a hundred days, waging war and bringing death and horror to Europeans until he was defeated at Waterloo in 1815. As my mother would have observed of Napoleon's rescue, it was one of those "more harm than good" situations.

Forgiving the great Newfoundland dog his good deed, I am reminded of the Ecclesiastical proverb, "A living dog is better than a dead lion." And today I am still in the business of ministering to my sick dog. I know, of course, that in trying to save Jody, I am, as usual, trying to save myself. I am indebted to her for her friendship and forgive all her own misdeeds over the years and so the characters in my novel will go unnourished while I go over and rub honey on her teeth until they shine like gold in the morning sunlight.

August 3

Glasswort, Orach, Sea Rocket

First let me tell you that Jody recovered. She became healthy again after at least two trips up to the front porch and barking at death's door. The door did not open. No one ever figured out what was wrong with her, though food poisoning or a very strong viral infection were considered. Possibly distemper. Yet, the thing that did not kill her did make her stronger. She actually seems healthier now than before she became ill. I am under the assumption that she has had one of those near-death experiences that lead people (and dogs) back into the world ready to live every minute for all it's worth.

At the bottom-most wrung, her eyes glazed over, she had ragged breathing and could not move. When I carried her she was a limp, lifeless bundle of dog. Now she barks at the garbage men with great gusto and chases flies in the house like a pup. I am still squirting liquid penicillin down her throat twice a day with a needle-less syringe. Maybe it was the penicillin that saved her.

Or it could have been the photograph of the old Pope that stood watch over her. Or it could have been the IV drip of saline solution that kept her from becoming dehydrated. "Dehydration is the real killer of old dogs and old people," Julia, the vet, said. So I am on guard against dehydration from here on.

Vet bills amounted to six hundred dollars and spare change. If I write about this incident and actually sell it for money, is the vet bill tax deductible? But who cares? Jody lived. I had a chance to believe in belief again and it sustained me ... and her.

At the lowest ebb of things, I remember lying on the living room floor where the dog had just vomited for the thirtieth time. I lay on the floor curled around my dog, comforting her and warding off death. And I succeeded.

Yesterday morning, walking across the front yard with bare feet, I stepped right on the back of the front yard snake. I landed square on him but he did not bite me. He slithered out from underfoot and went on his way. I saw this as a sign of great good luck. I went about my business and no harm came to me.

Later that day I went kayaking alone in Cole Harbour, a broad, shallow arm of the sea near here that I had not explored before. My kayak draws very little water so I can slide smoothly over the flooded islands of eelgrass and hear the sound of a thousand blades of this vital plant caressing the skin of my little boat.

It was late in the day and the sea wind was dropping. The water was warm, the sky blue, eventually turning to evening gold. A bald eagle flew over as if on cue. You smile at a moment like that and dip the kayak blade a little deeper, tasting the sweetness of life in the back of your throat. I would have started singing but couldn't think of anything to sing until something surfaced from my ribcage: "Sherry" by the Four Seasons. "Sher–err–y, Sherry Baby. Sher-err-y, Sherry, Baby." Fortunately, no one was around to hear my impossibly lame rendition of Frankie Valli. But for a slapdash instant, I was thirteen again and happy.

The eagle itself was dogged by a small crow. Eagles are almost always being chased by feisty smaller birds that want them out of their territories. I've watched the ravens dive at an eagle in front of my house. I've seen blue jays natter away at them, too, pestering their flight. Gulls swoop and peck at them in mid-air. And once, a brazen yellow-tufted sparrow chased a bald eagle above the marsh and out to sea.

Birds of prey abound in my corner of the universe. One of my pigeons – during the dark but hopeful days of the dog's recovery – was attacked by some bird of prey, likely an eagle or the greyish hawk that killed its mother and brother. The first sign of trouble was blood on the back steps. Pigeon blood looks exactly like human blood. The source remained a mystery until I found the limping, bleeding bird underneath my car.

I captured the injured pigeon, studied the wound: a gash under the wing, with the wing itself impossibly broken. I settled him into a small cage and taped his wing into place. My neighbour would point out to me that it seemed like there was one injured or sick animal after another all summer. It was that kind of a year. Demosthenes, the orphaned blue jay was coming along famously, although his tail feathers did not seem to want to grow in and he was reluctant to give up his begging and finger feeding. Clearly, he liked human attention, especially the flies I would swat for him.

The highlight of the paddle on Cole Harbour was my arrival at a nameless island where great blue herons roosted in the trees. No humans lived here, although I found the remains of a rustic house, swallowed up by raspberry vines and alders. The herons took to the sky as I arrived and I counted them twice. Thirty-three the first time, thirty-four the second, thirty-six the third time. They flew above me like a grey swirling tornado of wings. There was a crazy pattern to their flight since they were not flying away, just flying around. I had never seen this many herons all together, all in flight. I think of them as a soft-feathered version of pterodactyls, and perhaps they are. Back on the open water, I leaned back in my kayak and felt myself rising up into the sky. And then I paddled home against a stiff current beneath me that I could neither see nor understand.

The surface of the water was moving north but that was just the sea wind. Beneath, the harbour was draining south into the sea. I would slide easily over the clam-pocked shallows and then suddenly find myself in a narrow, deep channel with the current twisting me around in the opposite direction. While the surface water of the harbour looked more or less the same, beneath it were rivers of intense energy – tide work, moon work, ebb and flow of planetary powers. I let the currents teach me, sidling up to the invisible flood until I found the narrow, helpful back current that was going my way.

Cole Harbour is sprinkled plentifully with islands. My favourites are the small ones, some the size of my house, some the size of my Hyundai station wagon, some much smaller: the size of my desk, the size of me. Some islands in the harbour are nothing more than large cleft boulders with a ten-foot spruce tree on top, growing right out of the rock, sustained on God knows what – sheer willpower, lust to live, basic determination. A Mick Jagger kind of tree, angular, attitudinal, realizing that you can't always get what you want but if you try (some time) you just might find that you get what you need.

On such boulder islands, the tree does not stand alone. Brown and grey lichen are also growing from the rocks, some looking like small rectangular open books, lying flat with the edge of the tarnished pages curling up. And there are flowers too – stringy daisies and asters and the odd swaying devil's paint brush whipping back and forth on the large canvas of the evening air.

Alfred North Whitehead, a man whose intimidating name must have scared off girls when he was in high school, once said, "Life is an offensive directed against the repetitious mechanism of the universe." I think I know what he meant by that. It is a fight, after all. We are all struggling to survive; we are, in fact, struggling to do more than survive. We keep complicating what we "need" to survive. Our list of items necessary in the survival kit keeps getting longer as the new necessities grow larger, and more expensive.

Some days I think all I need is a white sheet of paper and a small window of the day in which to write. And that will be enough. But soon the page is filled with intelligible or unintelligible thoughts and I need to fill up my time with something more. The offensive continues. There is a battle, maybe, but I've never detected who the enemy is. White asserts it is the "repetitious mechanism." The life/death thing. The breathing in and out, over and over. The waking/sleeping issue. The three same meals a day. The being born, being young, being old, being dead. The raggedy Mick Jagger spruce tree on a God damn hard and uncomfortable rock that gives just enough of a platform for a living thing to hang onto life – until a hurricane comes or a lightning bolt or a hungry swimming porcupine comes along who wants to chew a ring around the bark to keep his own life going.

In the kayak in the harbour I was feeling okay about things since the dog was recovering and I only had a small list of disasters in my life I was keeping track of. Ahead of me was a season of considerable activity and confusion. There were deadlines, there were many repetitive, uninteresting tasks the universe was going to lob at me and I would duck and swerve and take a few hits on the chin or cheek.

I pulled up to the next island – a two-boulder affair with a small rim of stones around it. I could get out of my kayak and walk the entire perimeter of this island kingdom in less than ten seconds. There were no trees here but an assortment of inter-tidal plants that were edible: glasswort, orach, and sea rocket. I tasted each, decided the glasswort was the best, if saltiest, of the batch. A million snails lived among the small stones, the water slipping in and out of the tide each day in that relentless clockwork of moon tugging tide in and out.

Thomas Browne (who I had once liked nearly as much as *The Anatomy of Melancholy*'s Robert Burton) wrote a famous book in the seventeenth century called *Religio Medici* and in it he professes that "There is surely a piece of divinity in us, something that was before the elements, and owes no homage to the sun."

Out towards the ocean I could still see the vortex of herons. I had a small poem going in my head: pain, sorrow, regret, recovery, healing. This was my anthem of the evening. I would paddle to it as I made the last leg from my two-stone island to shore. I dipped the kayak paddle into the smooth dark water, the wind now no more than a girl's whisper in my ear, divinity in the swirl of days spiralling behind me, the ones whirling to come.

August 10

Affirm, Mature, Dissolve

"In stating as fully as I could how things really were, it was often very difficult and I wrote awkwardly and the awkwardness is what they called my style."

Ernest Hemingway.

I t started out as rain but I was certain it would clear. The wind was light out of the north, blowing from the centre of the province. I drove east again, this time to find the cliffs I saw detailed on the topographic map. Each foray into the wilderness this summer was an experiment of mind and body. No drugs, no booze, always just me, a map, a few books, a water bottle and a notebook. Seeking with an open mind for any detail – trivial or profound – that would capture my attention. I was doing what I had professed in my creative writing class last spring: "Write as if everything matters."

Stuck in road work on the Musquodoboit Valley Road, I turned off the car and began to read one of the books I had brought along. Trying to be eclectic, thinking I'd been relying too heavily on the Chinese, on the Zen, on the ancient, I had brought along Gustave Flaubert's *Madame Bovary*. I didn't last five pages before realizing that *Madame Bovary* would be no good for hiking into the forest. Flaubert was not the right companion for the hike along Pace's Lake. When the flag man gave me the go ahead, I threw *Madame Bovary* into the backseat where she would recline for several days before being rediscovered as I packed in my surfboard for a trip to the beach. Fresh crushed stones lifted by my tire tread pinged and popped underneath my car like sniper fire from the centre of the earth.

A turn off on a forgotten dirt road takes me to water. Ten minutes into the forest along Pace's Lake I come to the first cliff and at its base a jumbled mass of great squarish boulders, much like Devil's Bed on the northern end of Porter's Lake. I tuck into a comfortable den between several friendly, grey rocks and consider this cliff and rock pile thing as a great work of art: something formulated in the consciousness of the planet (I know, I know. Just sing with it for a minute). Cliff and rock pile, order and disorder. Flat face of a vertical cliff and the chaotic strewn mass of what was sliced and diced by the glacier when it passed through here and then again as it retreated. Pace's Lake.

I think of the advice of my parents: "Pace yourself," repeated often because I wanted to do many things too quickly, too soon or all at once. Time is nature's way of keeping everything from happening at once. Or making it seem that way, since everything really is happening at once. But if we lose the illusion of linear time, we may go mad. So today I pace myself.

Lichen, moss, and a morning lake of light now that the north wind (upon my instruction) has successfully persuaded the clouds to move south. I think there are small pools of time between some of these rocks. I study the shadows the sunlight creates. The old geometry teacher up in the sky today makes me name them: triangle, right triangle, isosceles triangle, hexagon, trapezoid, parallelogram.

Dipping into my backpack book collection at random, I discover that Claude Monet slashed more than two hundred of his paintings rather than turn them over to his creditors. Would a contemporary painter do this? Would a writer do the same? In graduate school I had learned that Fyodor Dostoevsky owed money too. He promised to write whole novels and owed them to his creditors with nothing to gain but getting himself out of debt. Dostoevsky's *The Idiot* was one possibility for today's book list but I turfed it from my pack at the last minute. Sitting alone in a forest with a dark book felt wrong. Another book about impressionists was considered but that too was left on the office floor in favour of one titled *Subtle Wisdom*, which has been a good companion. I added to it *Conquering Happiness* by Bertrand Russell because it was a slim old paperback (60 cents, new!). Added to that was a book called *Medicine Walk* by Laurie Lacey, a Nova Scotia author who I admire for his work on Mi'kmaq medicinal herbal plants.

Laurie Lacey suggests that when undertaking a "medicine walk" you should find a stone you like and see what it has to teach you. I believe that if I were to find the right rock it would teach me everything I ever wanted to know. Why is the sky blue? Why do fools fall in love? What happens when you travel beyond the speed of light? Is there life on other worlds? Why was Mickey Mantle such a great home run hitter? Lacey's other advice is that you should hike until you find a crow or raven and then pay careful attention to everything around you. I thought this was fine advice for the morning. This reminded me of my old pet, Jack, and of all the ravens in the world that I believed were watching out for me. So for today, wherever I found my black bird I would sit and write.

Hiking further along the forested shore, I discover the floor is a continuation of the rock jumble. Nothing is flat or fixed. Most everything is covered with thick moss but the footing is never certain. Some of the moss covers gaps and holes between the rocks and these holes are deep. It is tricky, calamitous walking with my feet twisting many directions as I try to continue onward. The trees above are calming and reassuring. I need to keep my eyes down but also ever upward, waiting for the crow or raven to appear.

The forest floor is an extravagant bed of thick moss and the jutting rocks sport crops of red-topped moon-men lichen; I think they are called "redcoats" because someone once thought they looked like miniature British soldiers. I recall from my history research that most British soldiers in the eighteenth century who found themselves in Nova Scotia detested the wilderness here. They wanted to be in England, back in a pub, not stumbling around the rocky floor of a forest with moss-covered holes big enough to swallow an eighteenth-century man.

There are rivers and streams of light flowing down to me through the gaps in the forest canopy, for the trees are tall and splendid here and it feels like a jungle. Not hot, but green and lush and dark beneath the leaves and needles. The hill above me to the east, I note from the map, is called Jerusalem Hill. The islands in the lake nearby are named Firebrand, Spark and Ember. There must have been a story there.

Also covering some of the exposed rocks is another form of lichen, the stuff used for miniature grey forests on model railroad tracks. It is quite exquisite, and plentiful. I wonder if the lichen is worth much. If it is, then the land beneath Jerusalem Hill is a gold mine of rail town miniature forests. That is, if there are still legions of model railroad enthusiasts out there in the world, bivouacked away in their basements.

Suddenly I can smell the smell of electric trains. "Affirm ourselves, mature ourselves, dissolve ourselves," is the natural progression of a man's life, says Master Sheng-yen, author of *Subtle Wisdom*, whom I had ignored up until now. I am of the opinion that I am still at work on the first phase of the three. But I consider the glacier that shaped this place. "Affirm, mature, dissolve." These things take time, I console myself. Maybe tens of thousands of years. I shift my focus from the trees to the moss, then study the shapes of the rocks beneath them, then refocus again and see what Monet would have me see – the space between the viewed and the viewer – and even that is full of several dimensions. Thin silversunned ribbons of spider webs and threads lacing together from moss peak to lichen outcrop. Each thread is an anchor for sunlight, a pale glowing rope. To focus on the extravaganza of spiderwork, you must stay very still and not breathe.

Alfred Stieglitz, addicted to the beauty of light, hated the hand-held camera at first, believing in the necessity of a rock steady lens in order to capture the beauty locked up in a thing or person. "Pace yourself," he might have said. To see a thing properly takes time and patience. Give the lens a chance to find what might otherwise be invisible. His favourite subject was his wife, Georgia O'Keefe, whom he photographed over and over for decades, something I would think would put a strain on any marriage. Sometimes, however, he photographed the skyscrapers of the city and beyond that what he called the "cloudscapes above."

That third state of one's development, dissolution, involves a disappearing act of self. It's the bodhisattva phase where one's total concern is with others, not self. Transcendence, no self-ness. The glaciers were a quick study compared to the rest of us.

No ravens or crows have found me here in the forest and this is a "working" trip that is a writing venture so I change the game plan. Whenever my foot slips into a pothole or crevice, I stop and write. By now I'm a rubber-ankled stone hopper but still the ground beneath me plans ways to make me write. Root tangle, snarl of low shrub, loose stones, wobbling rocks still not steadied by ten thousand winters. A hand pulls up from beneath the world and grabs my shoe. I fall spread eagled on a fat old round boulder.

"We are less bored than our ancestors were but we are more afraid of boredom," Bertrand Russell writes in *Conquering Happiness*. That is an attempt to explain why happiness was so difficult in the twentieth century. But how could one be bored on a morning like this?

And now each stumble, each event of false footing between the rocks is rewarded by whatever is to be discovered when I sit and look, read and write. Bertrand Russell reminds us that we have been on the run from boredom for centuries. Sometimes we fall and are swallowed by it. He's right about the fear aspect. Boredom is self-imposed exile from experience and the directive for exile usually comes from within.

I leave the inner forest and hike to the open shoreline – no shore really but a string of jumbled rocks of many sizes. I jump from stone to stone or clamber over the great boulders until I am directly across from Firebrand Island. I am now at the foot of the second, much higher cliff and I can sniggle my way up a seam in the rock, aided by credible roots and brushwork until I find a ledge from which I can see the whole of the lake. And here, barely within reach, is the first ripe blueberry of the year. The fruit is sun drenched and well ahead of the forest floor blueberry class of 2002. I pick it and savour the taste, then see others more accessible, but none as ripe or explosive to the tongue as the first.

The wind is moving on the water, making patterns of eternity. Three white rocks in the water look like the backs of Beluga whales. I spot three more dangerous blueberries and lust for them until satisfied. Further up the cliff is a small pocket of forest perched below an outcrop of rock. Another place to write. Spruce and pine needles fall on the page, wanting their stories to be told. I angle north to find a way up and attempt a smooth vertical face but soon admit defeat. A rope hangs from above – a long shank of clothes-line really, placed here as a temptation for a fool like me, suggesting, "This has been done before and we've left it for you."

Who tied the other end? Was the person reliable or reckless? What is the rope tied to? I decide to avoid the temptation. I begin a slow, sweaty climb down, feet ready to slide, fingers working seams and roots. On either side, unreachable, more blueberries test principles of risk/reward.

There is no easy route back through the forest and the bugs have heard the news of my fatigue. They assemble and begin their assault as I sip water and wait for inspiration.

A monk was once discovered peeing in a sacred hall before a golden statue of Buddha. A second monk was outraged and said, "You cannot pee here. The Buddha is here."

"Tell me where the Buddha is not so I'll pee there."

"But the Buddha is everywhere," said the second monk.

To which the first monk replied something to the effect, "So then I might as well pee here."

I pick a wilted fern for watering. Buddha stands watching from the bluff above me.

If I had continued to follow my plan to write at every time I stumbled into a hole, many, many words would have been spilled on the way back. So I changed plans and continued to wait for the ravens or crows to appear. None did. I was having trouble breathing and decided to settle into a kind of mossy hammock between big rocks with an army of mosquitoes that wanted to suck my blood as payment for safe passage back. Small collectives of anxiety – the unruly kind that come with sweat and hard breathing and fatigue – are gathering in the clouds above. There are deer flies along with the mosquitoes and black flies now and I wave my arms, then remember a nameless sage who pointed out that waving your arms attracts more flies and mosquitoes, like saying, "Hey it's me. I'm here. Come get me."

My car is hot and the road dusty. In the line-up of cars back at the road work, engine off, sweat crawling down the ladder of my spine, I drain what's left in my water bottle and look up to see my first raven of the day. His mouth is open from the heat and he is hopping from stone to stone on the hillside by the road work. He has no interest in me whatsoever. Two more ravens join him. They hover and they bob their heads and caw, something that sounds like a complaint to human ears but may not be that at all.

I toss a small left-over bit of doughnut to them but they aren't interested. They fly off, having reminded me of the three-fold path: affirm, mature and dissolve.

When I return home that morning, still sweating, I throw myself into the summer sea and feel the gentle tug of the warmest water of the year, pulling me away from shore in the rip current between the sand bars. It's a tease of danger, of course, and I swim against it easily to body surf a steep, breaking wave anxious to transport me safely back towards the sandy shore.

August 15

Halifax Walkabout

I'm calling this work, even though all I am going to do is walk around the city. There's a certain section of my novel, *Raising Orion*, that needs a specific background colour as my protagonist walks through a section of Halifax. So I want to get it right.

I park my car in the shade of a tree at Dalhousie University and set off with a pack, notebook, a bottle of water and good hard-working writer's intentions. I'm reminiscing about the small euphoria of my rainy, bug-infested morning by the Musquodoboit River, thinking if that pilgrimage was such a personal success, what about all the wide-eyed discovery to be had on this day, wandering at my own pace on a sun-dazzled summer day through a great historic city filled with people of every sort imaginable.

I check in quickly at my office at the Transition Year Program at Dalhousie and discover it is orientation day. Lunch is in ten minutes and I should show my face and give a small speech. I say that I'm too busy and then have to explain that what I'm doing is wandering around Halifax on foot for the novel I am writing and my director looks at me and says she wishes she could do that with her time. Patti Doyle-Bedwell is a wonderful Mi'kmaq woman who I admire and she's not being nasty, but truthful.

I walk out the door intending to waltz off down the street but run into the new recruits for TYP and get introduced to them by the assistant director, Isaac Saney. Isaac was recently tear-gassed by the police during protests when G7 finance ministers were in Halifax. He said it was quite painful but now he's back to work. I chat with the students and then decide I better at least stay for a sandwich and give my famous pep talk. This requires significant mental energy, firing up engines that I did not expect to ignite until September, and this is only August 15th. I switch the engines on and off as quickly as I can and soon I am back out the door. Heading east on University Avenue, under a fine summer sky, walking past the hospitals with their flowers all pink and blue in front.

I think of all the sadness behind those walls and windows and remember one year when I worked with a girl in the IWK hospital. She was dying of brain cancer and wanted to publish a book of writing by kids in the hospital. I was very encouraging and cheerful. The book came out and then she died. But other people continued to gather writings by kids in hospitals.

And that very hospital is where the scene from my novel begins with a middle-aged, second-hand bookseller and a fourteen-year-old boy who is dying of cancer and needs desperately to spend part of a day outside the four walls of his room.

At one of the nearby medical buildings, the covered body of a dead person is being wheeled off an ambulance and, presumably, headed toward a morgue. Two quite cheerful men who are wheeling the body are talking loudly about lunch.

There are trees shading me from the sun along University Avenue but when it turns to Morris, I put on my sunglasses. I take them out of my pack and discover my bug hood is still folded up in there – just in case. I cross the streets even though the lights are red. There's not much traffic. The sun is, by Nova Scotia standards, hot, and I notice that most other people are wearing sunglasses. This is the first of many disappointments.

When everyone wears sunglasses, you can't see their eyes and I like the eyes of strangers. I take off my own sunglasses – thin, alien plastic specs bought by my daughter in Arizona. I squint because the city is too bright. No one else is taking off their sunglasses and I know that wearing those damn pieces of plastic makes them feel isolated and aloof. No eye contact, but anonymity – just off on their way to wherever they are going.

That's when I come to the realization that nothing exciting, eventful or revealing has happened yet – twenty minutes into my adventure, my pilgrimage, and my research trip. Cynicism kicks in, and I think that without bugs and rain and a bug hat and a river, without thinking about Shirley MacLaine on the Camino, maybe nothing will happen here in the city. Full sun, people with sunglasses. A city is no good at all for this sort of thing.

I contemplate giving it up and getting out of the city to hike a spot on the map called Mount Misery. Certainly all kinds of good writing ideas would occur to me at a place like that. But I figure this is a kind of wimping out. I must plod on. Maybe something insightful will happen yet.

The Jazz Festival is on, three blocks to my left and, although it's not part of my character's path in the novel, I take a side trip there. People are sitting on lawn furniture out in full sunlight – all of them wearing sunglasses. The music on stage is coming from three university-age guys, somnambulant, who are playing very slow, spacey jazz. It sounds mostly like noodling on guitar and bass and a couple of slaps with the brushes on drums and it goes on and on. I would much prefer young and angry to this. Everything at this scene smacks of nice. I need out of there because I'm getting worried that this is about to be a very ordinary day filled with ordinary people and events – or non-events.

Cynically, I amble back down to Morris Street and continue on east towards the harbour. I pass by some brightly painted nineteenth-century houses, storefronts, a used clothing store, the Khin-Do. This is the small Vietnamese restaurant where a friend, my literary agent at the time, told me he was dying of AIDS and he wanted me to help him with some very important things before he died. I convinced him that he and I should write a powerful idealistic novel together and we got it started but then he began to go downhill. It was a save-the-world kind of novel that involved air travel and dolphins, I remember. And my agent friend, Peter, believed that Ted Turner should read it once it was finished. But it didn't get very far. Peter Livingston had been the son of the man who ran Capitol Records when they signed the Beatles. Peter had grown up around crazy and famous people. The Buddhists had brought him to Halifax and he had become a great hotshot literary agent in Canada. We became friends although we had come from very different worlds. He spent Saturday afternoons as a kid hanging out at the backyard pool in Los Angles with John Lennon and George Harrison. I had spent similar Saturdays at Lake Cotoxin swimming in dark cedar water with my cousins who were the sons and daughters of milkmen and bread men and salesmen of wall panelling.

When Peter died, he had a Buddhist funeral where I met his father and mother. I remember the Buddhists had really great vegetarian food there at the gathering afterwards. But our well-intentioned idealistic novel involving air travel and dolphins never did save the world.

In my current novel-in-progress, I had located Molly's Bookstore at "the forgotten end of Barrington Street." Now, as I approached the fictional store's location, I discovered it was not forgotten anymore. Now there was the Superstore here with its big asphalt parking lot baking in the sun. And there was a massive apartment tower under construction on what I had thought to be the most forgotten block of the street. My novel could no longer be totally contemporary because the city had changed. Reality was once again (as with the failed idealist novel) clumsily screwing up fiction and art. I wanted to make all this new stuff go away so that the street was the way I pictured it in my novel: used bookstore, a couple of shabby confectionary shops, the Lighthouse Tavern (the old strip-joint tavern) and a rundown laundromat. But they were all gone. The day was not turning out well.

I retraced my steps and wandered into the park across from the VIA Rail train station. A man crossing in my direction handed me a small flyer about September 11th. He was silent and hasty and I am glad he didn't want to preach to me. I sat on a bench and read the brochure – hell, why not. I'm in the shade and take my shoes off. Whenever I take my shoes off at a park bench, I remembered that in the old movies, someone would call their feet "dogs" and say something like, "time to give the dogs a breather." I give my dogs a breather and they thank me.

The hurried man's brochure, as I had expected, was about the end of the world. The Book of Revelations had predicted September 11th, it said, and it had also predicted "great weeping and wailing." Indeed. It said that in many nations, the "Antichrist forces are on the rampage, killing pastors and people." The author placed much of the blame on something referred to as "enchantment with drugs." Revelations had it all nailed down. But there was still time for one's soul to be saved before the big meltdown.

For such a small free brochure, I thought the printing job was pretty good. It reminded me, oddly enough, of my current novel, recently released after a long delay. And because of its delayed release, it seemed to be totally and categorically ignored. It had been advertised considerably, but the ads appeared a full year before it was released. People seeing it now for the first time thought it was already an old book. They thought it had come out last year and since they had not heard a word about it from anyone, they assumed it was a clunker. (These are my dark thoughts, anyway.) I think maybe I should get ambitious and hand out free pamphlets like the religious doomsayer. These pamphlets would have excerpts from the novel – brilliant little passages that would drive readers to the bookstores to actually buy those books now lingering on the shelves.

I picture myself acting like the hurried sweating man who I met in the middle of Barrington Street. I would try handing the excerpts of my novel to strangers – all wearing shades – and they would shun me, some thinking I was religious, some thinking I promoted escort services. I could see the little flyers littering the gutters and parks as pedestrians, too polite to refuse taking them from me, toss them unread.

But I don't think the life of a pamphleteer is right for me. I reject the idea and resign myself to the fact that my novel, six years in the making, will probably go entirely unread except for the one "fan" from Richmond, B.C., who tracked me down by Internet and sent me a lovely email saying how much she adored the book and would read others by me. I almost thought that the publicist at my publisher was trying to make me feel better by inventing the email, but there were quite a few typos and major grammatical errors so I think it was real. Towards the end, she admitted she had found the book in the library so there were clearly no royalties accruing from her love of the story. But her warm words were certainly appreciated and much better than "getting a stick in the eye," as fellow writer Harry Thurston would say.

I was beginning to feel that my urban pilgrimage was less than successful because nothing was really happening. I was wasting my time. "Better than a stick in the eye," though, I could hear Harry saying. And it was that.

So I tried to convince myself that I was reasonably happy if uninspired at my seat in the park. Men came out of the office building across the street – a shapeless, nameless government office building. They stood near me in the shade and smoked one, two or three cigarettes and then crossed the street and returned to their building. They were wearing laminated identification cards around their necks that I imagine label them as government employees and smokers. I don't mind the smoke drifting my way but I don't speak to them. I can tell that I am in a non-speaking mood, giving off vibes that tell people I'm no good at casual conversation. I'm like that most days but I do remember one day when a crossing guard who had grown up in Parrsboro was so desperate to talk of his passion for fishing, that he gushed praises for the fresh water fish of Nova Scotia for nearly a half hour to me, a total stranger willing to listen. I must have had my guard down on that day and it was worth it.

But today I sit here, resting my dogs, sucking in some second-hand government-employee smoke and realize I am at the park whose name I still can't recall, recently famous because the city had discovered a rare kind of beetle in the grass here. It was a foreign bug that had come in on the container ships nearby and spread no further than here. So they tore up all the sod and sent it somewhere to be stored. The park was nothing but dirt for a while and it blew all over the travellers heading into the bus and train terminals. New sod eventually covered the small desert and someday in the future, the papers said, they would tear up all this sod and bring back the original sod that would now be bug free. There were reasons for doing this, perhaps.

Beetles were becoming a problem in Halifax – what with trees being cut down at Point Pleasant Park and now more foreign beetles coming in on ships and wanting to devour the city. It just wasn't fair. The daily newspapers had nearly constant stories about citizens for and against cutting down park trees and others debating publicly about leaving or ripping up the sods. Maybe it was always like this in Halifax.

Elsewhere in the world, people are not nearly as concerned about sods and trees. At a nearby set of newspaper kiosks, I see three radically different front-page headlines. In one, life has been created from scratch for the first time in a laboratory. This has happened in Stoneybrook, New York, at the university I was once accepted at but never attended. Scientists have created, I read, a strain of polio just like the polio that ravaged the children of my generation before Dr. Salk's serum slam-banged the disease. If Stoneybrook scientists had to create life, I wondered, why not something – anything – other than a polio virus? Like the digging up, removing and returning of sods, there are probably reasons for this, reasons sifted out during meetings of committees of people who supposedly know what they are doing.

The *Daily News* shouts at me from the front page that way back on the infamous September 11th, the port authorities of Halifax Harbour had received reports that there was a hostile nuclear weapon in a container ship in the harbour. We were never informed of this until now, many months later. Sure, we knew about all the bugs leaping from the ships and coming ashore to ruin urban lawns and trees, but here was a supposed nuclear device designed to melt us down to human goo and we had not been informed. Lucky for us there had been no nuclear weapon.

I had once written a book about American nuclear weapons in Halifax Harbour. It was a kind of protest book, I guess you could say, designed to get other people more concerned about the nuclear arms race. I was planning to follow my own advice to work towards better East/West relations by mounting a goodwill surfing tour to the Pacific coast of Siberia. I was convinced, apparently, that surfing could help promote world peace but then the Berlin Wall fell and the Cold War ended, ruining my travel plans. I have always had a soft spot in my heart for anyone who worried about nuclear annihilation ever since my sixth-grade days of kneeling in the school hallway with my head up against the concrete wall and my hands covering my face to protect myself from radiation.

I am back on my feet, now, walking to the middle of the park with its new, temporary sods. In the centre is the statue of Edward Cornwallis. The last time I was here it was plastered with red paint – for good reason. Edward Cornwallis had left England with an entire contingent of English soldiers and civilians to start an instant city. He set off on May 14th, 1749, 253 years ago. It was one of those British military things, setting up a garrison town and preparing to fight the French yet one more time. Cornwallis was a bachelor of thirty-six, a man of cool demeanour at first but as the historian Thomas Raddall once noted, "Later on his voice acquired a rasp, and so did his pen, as trouble mounted and the harsh winters of the new colony destroyed his health."

I knew that Cornwallis didn't approach the challenges of Nova Scotia winter with the same positive attitude I did. But here he was immortalized in bronze, a founder looking tall and proud with his three cornered hat in his hand and his belief in England still rooted in his metal head. There was pigeon shit on both his shoulders and he had not a care in the world now that he was dead and his effigy was mounted upright in a resodded park.

The statue was surrounded by flat red bricks to walk on but one brick on each of the four sides – north, south, east and west – had been removed and someone had fit into each slot some kind of carved specialty brick of white concrete with a single word: "Sorry."

My guess is that this was some act of renegade commentary but I'm not sure by whom. You see, Cornwallis was also responsible, in his brutal and boneheaded military notions of civilizing Nova Scotia, for ordering Captain John Gorham to come up from Massachusetts to kill the native Mi'kmaq people. To wage war against them. And Cornwallis also offered a bounty for the scalps of Mi'kmaq men, women and children. In other words, he was a proponent of genocide. Mi'kmaq people today detest the thought of Cornwallis still being regarded as a prominent historical figure. That was why his likeness had been dashed with red paint more than once. And now, the small concrete apology (possibly placed here by his descendants) on four sides of him.

From here, I walk up Barrington a ways and then down to the harbour where more new apartment buildings have been built on a perfectly good piece of landfill that had once been cheap parking. I hike along the water's edge into throngs of tourists. The sun is still out and the wind light out of the north. Everyone is still wearing sunglasses and I'm feeling sour again, having dwelt too much on nuclear war, Edward Cornwallis, invading beetles and scientists bringing polio back to life. I drink often from my water bottle, convinced now that all this exposure to bright sun is leaving me desiccated. And there is no eye contact to be had in the world today.

The tourists are buying ice cream cones and paying for boat rides around the harbour. It's a little too precious and not like the Musquodoboit mosquito/black fly world at all. I can't sit down to write because I am sure nothing good will come from writing in bright sunlight. Curse the good weather. If I could only go up to people and introduce myself and try to get at what makes them tick, then I might get some good morsels of information, possibly a few anecdotes. But I own up to the fact that I am shy and have terrible people skills, so I go into a bookstore and sign some copies of my books. This, I suppose, to make me feel self-important. Inside I run into a former student with her fiancé, a young man from South Carolina and his parents up here visiting and someone saying to them, "You really should go to Prince Edward Island because it's so *nice* there."

My pen runs out of ink as I try to sign my books and I have to borrow one. I do try to be nice to the former student and her beau, but I realize I must flee this scene and that, truly, my day is a kind of bust: terribly ordinary with no profound moments. Just reminders of bleak history and cynicism taking up all the seats in the movie theatre of my brain. As I trudge off, I can feel the dark nemesis of depression stalking me.

I huff uphill, past the patio mid-day drinkers at Peddlers Pub, across the Grand Parade, once a marching ground for Cornwallis's soldiers in the days when there were still tree stumps in the middle of Barrington Street. There are more mid-day patio drinkers at the Economy Shoe Shop. I notice that they all are wearing sunglasses (of course) but that they all have notebooks or spreadsheets or, worse yet, palm pilots. They are getting on with their self-important lives and I have no idea why I am getting angry. Maybe I can't write in sunlight. I need fog and rain and bugs. I think about putting on my bug hood but, instead, I put on my sunglasses.

I stop in a store on Grafton, near the corner of a street named Blowers. Blowers is one of those names for a street that has often made people laugh. It's a good street for that, if nothing else. I wander into a store called the Black Market, which is worth my time because, in the novel-in-progress, the depressed Canadian history professor who has returned from nearly freezing

to death on Baffin Island is living in a rented apartment above the Black Market. Fortunately, from the outside it appears there is still a funky and rentable flat up there – windows open, wilted plants in the window. At least this building hasn't been torn down and turned into a condominium complex or a parking garage.

The Black Market is the store you would want to go to in Halifax if you ever needed incense, henna supplies, rain sticks, tie-died scarves, patchouli perfume or beads. They have hash pipes, too, and you'd expect they sold dope under the counter but I don't think they do. You could probably get a new screen for your bong, though, if you were really desperate and they wouldn't even charge you for it.

My sunglasses were off and I was getting a little weepy from all of the incense. The place was crowded with young people. I wanted to strike up a conversation with someone in there, to tell them that a character from my novel "lived upstairs" but I knew my people skills were at an all-time low level so I kept my mouth shut.

There are times like this, that I do say things to strangers and it comes out pretty weird. I go to say "Nice day," and it sounds like "Ice tray" and they wonder what planet I am from.

So it's back out into bright sunlight and past skateboarders not skateboarding today but looking bored as they finger the wheels on their skateboards. I take the diagonal route across the front of the public library and note that Winston Churchill is still frozen there as a statue with as much pigeon shit on him as on Cornwallis, although I don't think Winston deserves it. Churchill once said, "When you have to kill a man, it costs nothing to be polite." I'm pretty sure he was talking about Hitler at the time. Churchill was a man who also said flatly that his "rule of life prescribed an absolutely sacred rite of smoking cigars and also drinking alcohol before, after and, if need be, during all meals and in the intervals between them."

So, good for Halifax to erect a statue of Winston here so I can see it on this ordinary day for I am already in retreat. I head back to the university, up Spring Garden Road, past fashionable stores, feeling completely unlike Churchill who felt he had "been walking with destiny."

I zig off my homeward path ever so slightly to tack through the Public Gardens. Although most people find this park wonderful with its exuberant summer flora, mallard ducks in the muddy pond and fancy bushes and cactus garden, I find that the Public Gardens always makes me tired and unambitious. It's all so cultivated and Victorian and quaint and they close it down in the winter because, well it's winter. And it's full of sunglasses and tourists and mothers pushing little kids in those new expensive prams that you can use even if you are jogging.

I sit down on a bench and let my mind go numb while looking at roses, so I almost miss it at first. The uniformed security guard, an old grandfather type in a blue cop shirt, black pants, and hip-hitched walkie talkie, is walking towards a beautiful young woman who has seated herself in front of some peonies and pulled down the top of her dress.

"Not allowed," I hear him say.

"Not allowed?" she repeats.

"No." Grandfather Guard is saying this like it happens every day. He's hanging onto his walkie talkie (in case he needs back up?) and he shows no expression at all. He is not being nasty or friendly, just professional. It's as if he's been specially trained for just this sort of crime.

I don't want to stare but it's hard not to look. Nobody else in the park seems to notice. She pulls her dress back up over her delicate shoulders and gets up. I linger – just to see how this will play out. I stay seated on the bench and, fumbling for something purposeful to do, take out my notebook and start writing.

She angles in my direction as she is leaving the park and I judge her to be nineteen or twenty, university age, with long wheat coloured hair. I really would like to talk to her because there must be a story to her act of – whatever it was. She looks slightly embarrassed and I wonder if she is simply European and she thought this would be no big deal to sit in a public place in sunlight by the peonies and let your top down. Or was it something more important than that – a dare to herself, a commitment to public nudity? Certainly not mere exhibitionism. Unfortunately for me, my conversational skills are still at an all-time low.

"Hi," I say to her as she walks behind me. "Too many rules," I add, wishing I had Churchill's gift of language to say something important and clever but not insincere.

She smiles at me and she seems a little confused in a youthful, naive way and I still would love to hear her story but she walks off behind me on the grass and, as I turn to look at her, I see that she is meandering, drifting one way, then another, actually circling a pine tree, before heading for the exit to the Public Gardens.

The security guard is talking to the gardeners and he is shaking his head. I don't know why, but I feel pleasantly surprised and rewarded that even here in the Victorian stronghold of a previous century, a small cultivated haven of rules and regulations and force-fed flowers and Wonder Bread ducks, someone performed a lovely deed of nonconformity.

Outside the Public Gardens, there is an old man on a bench, a busker or a beggar with his head leaning against his accordion. He seems to have just fallen asleep. His hand is still attached to the accordion billows as it drops down to his side and the accordion sounds one long, sad chord that is quickly drowned out by the busses going by on Spring Garden Road.

August 24

Slugs and Space

Mars is closer to the earth than it has been in 60,000 years, but it is morning and I cannot see the red planet. Tonight I will look up into the sky with my binoculars and search for the canals. I know they are there despite the data coming back from the Mars missions.

When I was a boy of twelve, enamoured with space and science fiction, I was certain I would visit Mars before I died. Now I know I will not visit Mars. We don't even have those jet backpacks promised to us and our cars have no anti-gravity devices. Spaceships are faulty and explode. Just yesterday, Brazil tried to hoist itself up into space with a rocket and it exploded, killing twenty. Brazil, with its legions of starving street kids, pouring its money into space. Following our lead.

Meanwhile, I sit down on my back porch alongside my most recently adopted injured bird. This one is a young grackle that I have named Boethius. I read a bit from Annie Dillard's *Teaching a Stone to Talk*. An inch worm appears on the spine of the book and performs that amazing dance, groping out into space with the first half of itself until it finds purchase, then landing with its front "feet" and telling the back half of the body that it is okay to come on along. I have no idea how this wondrous creature arrived to steal me away from the text but it has and it goes first one way down the spine and then back, examining the book twice and then trying to figure out what to do next.

Much like me. Much like the rest of us. Even those who want to go into space. Send a fragment of humanity, bit by bit, up there and then eventually drag the rest of us along to God knows where. But, sadly, I will not get to the moon or to Mars in this incarnation.

Boethius is eyeing the inchworm and, for an instant, I consider offering the bird the feast but quickly change my mind and settle the trooper back into the grass. Live long and prosper.

A fellow writer from Kenora, Ontario, dropped by yesterday and we discovered that we are on similar quests. Pete Sarsfield is a doctor who works in remote northern communities and he is a writer who is seeking to find connections in seemingly random observations and events in his life. So am I, I tell him. We are both a bit surprised. We are not writing books about cancer or carbon dating or space travel or about other writers. We are scraping away at the surfaces and the insides of everything we encounter. We are bumping about trying to figure things out. And have mutually come to no solid conclusions. Which is where we both want to be.

And we're convinced, damn it all, that we are getting somewhere and writing good stuff and that there are no ultimate conclusions. Only workable truths along the way.

Soon Pete is off to Digby and the Balancing Rock on Long Island and so we diverge on our voyages of discovery. One of us is on the *Beagle*, I suppose, with Charles Darwin, while the other is wishing he had lived the life of astronaut John Glenn. We've paid our fare and want our money's worth from the tour.

According to Annie Dillard, an Irish archbishop, James Ussher, declared that the world began in the year 4004 BC. This was a religious idea, a seventeenth-century idea. Ussher was off by several million years but he at least tackled a difficult prediction and gave it his best shot.

If forced to make predictions about the future this morning, I would guess that the world will get a bit worse before it gets better. And then it will get worse again but some good will come from trials and tribulations. Meanwhile, the inchworm will have forgotten about his expedition down the spine of a book. He will not remember the gentleness of my own fingers as I plucked him carefully and set him back in his world of weeds and grass. Whatever happened to him probably makes no sense at all and adds no new meaning in his universe, or at least, his version of the universe. And Boethius is still staring at me with one grackle eye, wondering why I am sitting near his cage if I am not there to feed him a slug (his favourite) or a blueberry picked on the hill or at least offer up a leftover piece of corn on the cob.

I had to stand to shake out some ants crawling up my pant leg as I continued an inner debate with myself as to which trees around me were black spruce and which ones white spruce. I reminded myself how little Nova Scotians appreciate the beauty of spruce trees, which are considered to be low-class trees, truly growing like weeds, crowding each other out as if they didn't have the good sense God gave living things. The spruce is a tree that sheds its needles far too quickly if you take one inside for Christmas. (But I have stubbornly used one from my back lot each of the twenty-some years I've lived on this coast and always vacuumed up the needles with good humour, knowing another year had passed, and I had cut my own tree, making a good sacrifice of one so the others around it could grow tall and full.)

The trouble with sitting on a hillside with a notebook in hand is that it announces to the insect community that you are up for grabs. I did go on a short killing spree of mosquitoes and felt little guilt. Clearly, I was becoming the centre of attention there and the audience would have to pay for it. But not the ants. Not one bit me so I just had to stand every few minutes to shake them out of the pant leg.

A quick inventory of the plants around me revealed Labrador Tea, cranberry and blackberry, ground juniper, pigeon berry, Indian pear, black spruce/white spruce, one lone spindly maple tree and some wild spirea. And then the mosquitoes won the war on who should be spending the morning on this hillside above the Atlantic.

Later that morning, in the garden, I undertook a bit of a slug-tossing event (a slugfest, of sorts), plucking the little beasts off my tomato and zucchini plants and heaving them into the salt marsh. I assume most survive the toss, landing on soft grasses before collecting their thoughts and going back about their business. There were likely a few that would end up more vulnerable to birds and I would not grieve their demise in another food chain linkage.

A slug, as you probably know, is pretty much a lower-class snail without the gratification or protection of a shell. It wreaks havoc with a garden with its hunger and it leaves leftover slime, which can rot a good cucumber in a day. Evolution did not think slugs needed shells. They have no wings so when I toss them, they do not fly. A biology text points out that the slug's anus is near its mouth, which sounds like another adolescent joke on the part of evolution and I was not pleased to learn this, having once kissed a giant West Coast slug on Vancouver Island at the bidding of some sixth graders who suggested I should try this before going back East.

Slugs move by "a rippling motion of an elongated foot" and they are of the class Gastropoda, which means "stomach-foot" and boasts more than 40,000 species. How did the planet get so many of the little bastards anyway?

Recent news events had me pondering world affairs again, against my better judgement. Sometimes I take things rather personally. After several years, for example, I was still having a hard time reconciling the fact that the U.S. (where I was born and raised) and its allies were responsible for the death of a half million Iraqi children in the Gulf War. I stopped tossing slugs that now seemed to deserve no more punishment and went to the beach.

"If nothing lay more developed, the quahaug in its callous shell were enough," said Walt Whitman in *Leaves of Grass*. He was perfectly happy to forgo the rest of evolution, including the part that included humans, and he would still find the scheme of life quite grand. Too bad the Americans had not chosen Walt Whitman as a national hero and followed his celebratory advice. Instead of dropping bombs on civilians, Americans could be spending their days and their dollars cheering on the small songbirds and encouraging flowering weeds to grow or congratulating the molluscs and patting themselves on the back (as Whitman did) for their own good fortune to have a body worth singing about ("I Sing the Body Electric") and a natural world to walk around in. Whitman is also the poet who said, "And as to you Corpse, I think you are good manure, but that does not offend me." What a great attitude towards one's death.

In the shallows at the beach, I detected one of several small holes in the sand and forked my fingers down on either side, drawing up a small clam, not as grand as an outright quahaug, but a clam nonetheless. It was turning into a molluscan kind of day and that was good enough for me. Everyone in the phylum Mollusca has "a muscular foot, a visceral mass and a mantle." This seemed like a good description of some teachers I had in high school and certainly some had teaching styles to match, but that was all many years ago. In fact, it had been there in a biology class (with an exceptionally bright and entertaining bi-pedal teacher) that we had once dissected a clam. Whitman would have been outraged.

It was the same biology teacher, Mr. Muldova, who explained to his Cinnaminson High School students that the only reason our nation was then fighting in Vietnam was to protect the tapioca fields. He didn't like the war, nor did many of us, but he thought there was a lot of American money invested in tapioca plantations there and our government was over there in Southeast Asia slaughtering civilians in order to protect the tapioca corporations. He was the only person I had ever heard put this theory forward and many in class believed him to be correct although I never bought into it.

Clams, quahaugs, slugs, snails and even squids are all in the great big Mollusca phylum and not one of the members of that club had done any significant long-lasting damage to the planet, so I was thinking them a bit more noble than my own brood. Clams were in the class called bivalves, as Mr. Muldova had instructed and he noted that most bivalves were "suspension feeders," which reminded all of us of certain classmates devouring their lunches in the cafeteria.

As I recall, there were two people to a clam during the dissection day when the room smelled sweetly of formaldehyde and I was paired up with Kathy Kurtz. I had a crush on her even though she was interested in football players and I was not of that phylum. Being the guy, I did the cutting and Kathy Kurtz told me how much she was in love with Tim Stack but of course Tim Stack, the school football quarterback, was not interested in her. This was the sort of thing often discussed during clam dissection in those days and I was a sensitive listener.

Together, Kathy and I, with the help of a workbook, made an illustration of the innards of that clam and titled it "Anatomy of a Clam." I drew the picture but her handwriting was neater than mine and she labelled all the parts: gill, foot, pulp, mouth, gut, colon, heart, adductor muscle, anus. In the handbook it noted, "Bivalves have no distinct head."

Only Dan Stosuy was foolish enough to try to eat his clam after dissecting it and he got sick and threw up soon after that, much to the chagrin of Mr. Muldova and the rest of us. I never did reveal my attraction to Kathy Kurtz to her and she never dated Tim Stack, who grew up to be a banker.

I studied the small, living North Atlantic clam in my hand and decided he needed to get on with his life so I dug him a new home closer to the water line and placed him back in it, while the ghost of Walt Whitman cheered from the sidelines. "All things of the universe are perfect miracles, each as profound as any."

There on the beach, I had also been thinking about a young seagull that kept attacking his own reflection in a high window at my house. The pounding of the gull on the glass often sounded like someone was renovating upstairs, taking a hammer to the wall, and my daughter thought it was me up there building something while I was actually off surfing, or tossing slugs or reading about molluscs.

I thought I spied the bashing gull there on the beach rooting through McDonald's and Tim Hortons bags that he'd stolen from the trash can. The gull had his own reasons for bashing at my window, I am sure, but I talked to him (or his look-alike) and told him to cut it out. I even opened up the Tim Hortons bag and gave the gull a couple of leftover Timbits which he accepted without any sense of gratitude whatsoever. It did the trick, though; the gull did not return to bash at the windows.

The dunes at my beach at Lawrencetown are a nesting area for plovers and there are signs suggesting we be kind to this dwindling, endangered species. They spend some of the summer here humping and hatching and eating bugs and racing along the shoreline on these spindly cartoon legs. Then they are off to South Carolina or beyond for the winter. If we are not careful, however, they won't be around for the next generation.

Since the beach was empty, the plovers were working the shoreline in groups. If one was startled and flew, they all flew like one big arm of birds before returning to settle near the same spot to continue feeding. I decided to leave them alone and wander the dunes, keeping an eye out for plover eggs and nests. Though I think most had hatched by now, with the entire tribe gobbling bugs in preparation for the long migratory flight south. This is much like me, consuming a large quantity of food before an airplane flight, now that free meals are not served aboard Air Canada any longer. If the plovers were headed for Orlando, they knew enough to pig out before taking off, just in case there was no food cart on the way.

In the dunes I heard the song of what I believe is a white-crowned sparrow. Sparrows don't look like much but they always have great anthems. This particular sparrow is said to learn a specific song during a "sensitive period" in its youth, then "improve" upon it during a juvenile phase until the tune "crystallizes" into one final, single song that the bird sings for the rest of its days. You could argue that some people are like that. And it's either a wonderful melody or it's the same damn crappy song over and over.

Other species of songbirds like the finches and canaries have a different musical attitude. They learn a "sub-song" not long after they hatch and turn it into their own song by the end of their first year. After that, they do riffs; they improvise on that first song until it becomes new and improved. This happens year after year and the bird's unique personal song keeps evolving through an entire life. They call it "open-ended learning," which is quite nice if you think about it. I'm all for open-ended learning.

At the lowest point of the tide of the day, I waded into the rocky pools near the point of the headland and went about a lifesaving mission for starfish. Some starfish don't seem to understand that if they choose a pool too high up near the shoreline, they will desiccate and die when the water drops. Someone will argue that this is a clever Darwinist way of improving the species. The dopey starfish die and the bright ones live on. It is another kind of lesson altogether, certainly the opposite of open-ended learning. A starfish probably has only one shot at making a good choice in where to be at low tide. High and dry and dead or tucked into a briny wet spot down lower, still covered in sheltering rockweed if not seawater itself.

I for one think this unfair, as do my daughters who in their youth helped me rescue as many starfish and jellyfish that the sea had tossed up for dead. I still continue with the tradition. Creatures that make mistakes deserve at least a second chance, if not a third one or a lifetime of them. I know that I have been fairly heartless with slugs, but starfish seem different, thanks to the mythology of children's picture books.

Just to put this in perspective, let's leap up the evolutionary scale and assume man is either slug or starfish. And just for the sake of argument, consider that God (if God exists and we would like Him to, even those of us who doubt His credentials and His wisdom) thinks somewhat like me.

God is either tossing us like slugs in the wind, out of the garden, or He is taking pity on our foolish mistakes and trying to put us all back into the water for a second chance. We would love to convince Him that, like the finches, we want to continually learn to improve upon the song we learned in the nest. We want to be more than a clam dissected in a high school biology lab. We want to avoid bashing at our own image in windows but we can't help it if we keep crawling up God's pant leg thinking it is a way of getting into heaven. We know that if we become too annoying we get swatted by a reflexive hand and become a smudge on the face of God. But we need forgiveness. We need more time to evolve and in our open-ended learning scheme, it seems we have to make every conceivable mistake before we can move on. It's just gonna take a little more time.

So we're begging for patience.

September 10

Blasts from the Storm Centre

In 1959, when I was eight years old, I liked to dig underground forts and did a poor job covering second base according to my Police Athletic League coach. I mailed away for magic items including whoopee cushions and stink bombs. I also learned that there were big problems in the world because I watched the news on TV and wondered why all the adults were too stupid to fix things up. I was pretty sure that, if given the chance, I could establish world peace by the time I was twelve. That is, if I stayed focused and didn't get distracted by girls.

My father, coming home tired after working on milk trucks every day, could fix the chain on my bicycle and the broken hinge on the chicken coop. I never asked why he couldn't go out and fix the world by achieving world peace. I guess I instinctively knew that fixing the problems of the world was different from fixing the chicken coop. Besides, my father had already participated in the Second World War where his job was fixing military trucks and jeeps all over England, France and parts of Africa. That was his stint at achieving world peace – by way of automotive repair.

At eight, some bad things had happened to me. I stepped in dog shit a couple of times because I wasn't looking at where I was going. This seemed, at the time, incredibly stupid of me – or maybe

I thought of it as bad luck. My timing was bad: I stepped in dog shit once on my way to church; I stepped in dog shit once just before I got on the school bus. The latter was worse. During religious ceremonies, people who smell dog crap keep their ideas to themselves. On a school bus at eight in the morning, kids are every vocal about how they feel about the smell. They assigned blame. It was hard on a young man's spirit.

Other bad things had happened. I fell from a Tarzan rope into Steele's Pond – but was only mildly injured. My pet turtle died. I encountered personal setbacks in terms of male/female relation-ships. Girls liked me then dumped me, all before the age of nine. I was a laggard at math but I had decided that kids who were good at math led uninteresting lives. I made a thorough study of this amongst my classmates and it seemed obvious.

I lost some of my favourite baseball cards while "pitching" them. Sometimes it was called "flipping" cards. You and your opponent, in my case Whitey Posniak, would compete by throwing, sort of sliding, your cards along the floor towards a wall. If you topped another card you won it. I lost Roger Maris and Mickey Mantle in one fell swoop when Whitey topped them both with an Ernie Banks card. His name really was Whitey by the way – at least his nickname. It wasn't like some Black kids had named him Honkie or Cracker. He had blond hair so he had become Whitey by age four. If he had a real first name, no one knew it. Today those lost cards would be worth a considerable sum of money. More than I've earned for several of the books I've written. I grieve even now.

Now I know this all must sound trivial to those of you who led classically tragic lives as children. I apologize. It's just that I rolled along fairly smoothly in those bucolic days. I slept well in a room my father carved out of the attic. My brother snored in the bed across the room but he claimed that he didn't. He said I snored and I claimed it was a lie. We sometimes argued about this and fought and if we were really unruly, my father or my mother hit us on the butts with a belt. In those days, getting smacked by a belt on the ass was considered a good form of discipline. Most of my classmates got the belt for one thing or another except for Bobby Yeager. His father would strip off his clothes, poor gasoline on them and light them on fire. Bobby Yeager's father had his own school of discipline.

So, I survived the lashings and the public humiliation in buses and churches, being scarred by the fickleness of young girls who favoured then rejected me, living through the loss of cards portraying home run hitting baseball players and even the cancellation of some of my favourite TV shows: *My Friend Flicka, Leave it to Beaver* and *Howdy Doody*. (I remained loyal to Howdy long after the show had ceased to broadcast.) And then I turned my sights to larger issues of the day, like world peace.

Dag Hammarskjöld wrote an interesting, thoughtful and somewhat autobiographical book of musings called *Markings*, which was very impressive but nearly unreadable. He had been Secretary General of the UN when I was growing up until he died in a plane crash. I thought he was a neat guy because of the sound of his name and because he was Scandinavian. He worked for world peace, which I very much approved of when I was eight years old.

Unfortunately for all of us, we were in the midst of something called the Cold War, and that was a puzzling war indeed. Tensions built between the United States and the Soviet Union and we all waited to go to nuclear war. One of my fears was that some idiot would start pushing those red buttons before I got old enough to straighten things out. Old enough was twelve. At eight, twelve seems like adulthood. From eight to twelve is a long stretch of your life. If my math is right it means that you are adding four years onto your life – equivalent to half the life you already lived if you follow my drift. Each year, of course, gets shorter after that, until seasons blink by in the great time rampage of getting older.

I can remember springtime where I grew up being a time of great blooming skunk cabbages that grew down by Pennsauken Creek. I can remember muddy water and the creek washing in old tires and garbage that drifted in with the tides coming inland from the Delaware River. The skunk cabbages and the tidal junk were both very attractive to me for some completely unknown reason. If I had been a young Van Gogh, this is what I would have painted. I paid close attention to the details of the natural world and the artistry of tidal garbage and I watched a lot of bad television.

I believed in *The Three Stooges* like it was a religion. Curly was my favourite Stooge. I could never understand why some kids thought Moe was their favourite: he was shrewd but cruel and that was unacceptable to a person like me who was in favour of world peace. Larry, with the big hair, seemed unethical. He got away with whatever he could get away with. Curly, bald and naive and childlike, was an exemplary Stooge even though he was always the victim.

When you grow up in the 1950s, you remember *The Three Stooges*. You don't remember historical details like the death of Stalin and the rise of Khrushchev and $50 billion in foreign "aid" spent by the American government. If I had been growing up in Canada I probably would have paid even less attention to the opening of the National Library and the Pipeline Debate; I would have been impervious to the squalling of Lester Pearson and John Diefenbaker.

Those of us who grew up on the East Coast in the 1950s all remember Hurricane Hazel. The year was 1954. It was the first great hurricane of my youth and it blew down a lot of trees and wreaked havoc on the Jersey Shore. It even hit Toronto on October 15th. My parents claim I slept through most of it. After all, it was nighttime and I was only three years old. But I assume they are lying to me because I remember the lights going out. We had been prepped by the news on the radio for this to happen. We still lived in the trailer in those days. I think that when you are small, a trailer is a great place to live because it is small too, and it makes for a cozy little world. Later, when you are big, you can move into a bigger place called a house – which my father was building while we lived in the trailer.

In the morning after the hurricane, with my three-year-old eyes, I surveyed the catastrophe: tree limbs down everywhere; some whole trees uprooted and slammed down across the roads. Power lines down. A wild, wet sunlit morning after a big tropical storm: what could please a lad more?

I'm sure a lot of important stuff happened between Hurricane Hazel and me turning eight. But it's going to take deep hypnosis to bring much of it back. All I know is that, by 1959, I was eight years old. The St. Lawrence Seaway opened that year even though I wasn't paying attention. Castro overthrew Battista in Cuba. I missed that one too. Something involving communism was going on in China and the adult Americans didn't understand what that was all about.

Before he ended up in a fiery death falling from the sky in a plane over Africa, Dag Hammarskjöld wrote in *Markings*, "The anguish of loneliness brings blasts from the storm-centre of death." I don't think I knew loneliness as a child. It was an invention of adolescence, when I suddenly began to care about what other people thought of me, and realized that most of them didn't care one way or the other. They either didn't know who I was – all those revolutionaries in China, all those followers of Castro, all those unruly Russians, even all those beautiful girls wearing long white socks over their bare legs going to the Catholic school up on Route 130 – or they had sized me up and found me most ordinary.

By the time the sixties rolled into my neighbourhood I was in the process of inventing my own form of heroic loneliness as only an adolescent boy can. In 1963, I turned twelve years old. That was the year I was supposed to achieve world peace. I was at the end of my four-year plan for preparing myself to change the world for the better. My grandiose plans were rarely ever spoken to anyone out loud, but they were part of a private good-willed fantasy.

The world had become a more ominous place by 1963 because I was more aware of what was going on around me. The skunk cabbage still bloomed in the spring. The garbage floated in at the higher tides. Had I grown up with Dag Hammarskjöld for a father or had I been placed in some remote monastery for young idealists, I might have had a few clues as to how to go about achieving world peace. Instead, I had to rely on what I was being force-fed by television and by what I learned in social studies class. China was invading India, North and South Vietnam were tearing away at each other in a war that would drag some of my childhood baseball-card-collecting friends to their deaths. To the north, Canada was hanging its last criminal, opening up the TransCanada Highway and introducing Medicare. But all I had been taught about Canada was that it looked like a big pink country sitting on top of the United States. We would wonder, if we wondered at all, why they didn't just join us and become Americans so we could own the North Pole.

Also in 1963, China had an earthquake and only 25,000 people were killed. Ten times that many had died in Antioch, Syria, two years before while I was ten years old and improving my ability to hold down second base.

By twelve I was losing interest in baseball, a sad thing because baseball was something I could believe in. I knew it wasn't really important but I believed in it anyway, and it's usually better to believe in something rather than nothing.

I was wading into the great murky waters of adolescence, or whatever it is that feels cold and solitary and draws you into it. You tiptoe at first into the cold clammy water of the dark muddy river. Then you move forward and you see there are skunk cabbages blooming on the banks. The water comes up to your knees and you think you can still turn back if it gets too weird. Then the water is up to your thighs. By the time the water is up to your crotch you know there is no turning back.

You either dive into it then, or you continue to shuffle slowly ahead until it reaches your neck. I think I shuffled. I was cautious about some things. When entering cold water for a swim, the quick dive is a rude awakening, a sharp pain of cold followed by exhilaration. The slow descent elongates the drama and the discomfort, if not the pain.

In W. H. Auden's introduction to Dag Hammarskjöld's *Markings*, he writes, "To be gifted but not to know how best to make use of one's gifts, to be highly ambitious but at the same time to feel unworthy, is a dangerous combination which can often end in mental breakdown or suicide." He was hinting, perhaps that these were real challenges for Hammarskjöld himself. Fortunately for me, I came from a family that did not expect their progeny to have "great gifts" or be highly ambitious.

Some basic ambition was good but climbing beyond your family's expectations was bad. It got you into trouble. It led to a fall. My parents would urge me to go to university but they turned cool over my notions of graduate school. As if to say it was overreaching. Education was a good thing but too much education – well, that could really mess you up.

Between those crucial four years of eight to twelve, I maintained the desire to save things: pigeons drowning in the creek, dogs hit by cars, snakes foolishly lying on the warm summer macadam of the roadway. Boys must get this savior idea from movies or TV or even the church or from their own self-important notions of who they are.

My great disappointment at twelve years old, up to my Adam's apple in the cold muddy water of adolescence, was that I had held to my belief that I really could save the world from war, from murder and from cruelty if only given a chance. But I honestly didn't have a game plan. I was a kid who wrote poetry and bad science fiction stories about encounters with aliens. I sneaked lustful glances at the women modelling the underwear in the Sears catalogue. If I was lucky, I kissed a girl once every three months.

I had strong opinions. Many of them were not really my opinions but just hand-me-downs. Some of my opinions changed dramatically, sharply, in opposite directions once I began to make proper use of my brain cells. The Vietnam War is probably as good an example as any. I started out with the opinion we were getting involved to save the Vietnamese. TV news changed all that.

Paying attention to the big problems of the world led to confusion on a massive scale. What exactly would I do now to save the world? Now that I knew how complicated a mess it really was. It wasn't anything I could discuss with my friends or potential girlfriends. (Most of them remaining *potential* that year.) In the Moravian Church that I attended there is a giant mural painting at the front of the church of Jesus Christ walking through the Valley of the Shadow of Death and he is carrying a lamb. It's a wonderful, gentle painting of a sad-looking guy with a beard leading a flock of sheep through a valley in the Middle East. Something that looks like Hurricane Hazel is brewing in the background. The look on his face shows that he knows he is like the lamb he carries, something that will eventually be sacrificed. He understands the relationship between compassion and martyrdom and the painter has captured this ultimate sad conclusion in the face of Jesus.

In fact, the martyr idea was an attractive one to me at around twelve. But, fortunately, I couldn't see how the sacrifice of me could do anybody any good. But having gone through my own ineffectual, mopey and unfocused version of youthful martyrdom, I can at least understand how easy it would be to convince a twelve-year-old boy to be a suicide bomber if he thought he was going to do some "good."

I envisioned launching myself in front of a school bus, perhaps, in order to save a girl I had a crush on. My favourites were beautiful but sad girls. In my imagination, I was diving in front of nearly a dozen school buses a week to save those sad but beautiful ones. Why it was always a school bus is anybody's guess. I suppose because it was large and yellow and would attract more attention to the martyr. And, of course, I wanted lots of credit and attention for my deed. All this would happen after I was dead. Somehow, the fact that I would not be around for the girl to peck me on the cheek or for the mayor to applaud my good deed did not tarnish the lustre of the idea.

In my science fiction stories, I sometimes used mind control to make people good. To stop soldiers from killing. To eradicate nuclear weapons. It worked every time. I (or my fictional character) was good at it. Often, however, he made sacrifices to do so. He had no social life (like me sometimes), he was unrecognized for his great gift to humanity (like me again) and he was ostracized when people did not believe that world peace was the result of his actions.

The Berlin Wall was a year old and standing firm. Vietnam kept getting bloodier and uglier. The U.S. government was steamed up about Cuba. Rachel Carson was publishing *Silent Spring,* pointing out that we were systematically killing the living things on the planet. The economy was booming and I had the leisure to sit around berating myself for the fact that I couldn't save the world from itself. Not until I was much, much older, and only then if I could keep cynicism at bay.

It was this realization, this so-called wisdom of my age, that made my knees buckle. I was up to my chin. I could smell the water and knew it to be dirty and polluted, fed by industrial pollution and raw sewage. But I couldn't help myself when I slipped under. I held my breath. I did not open my eyes. I longed to be somebody else, someone with different, even lesser, ambitions. I stayed there beneath the surface for as long as my lungs would allow. Then I burst up through the surface, back into the same world I had left.

Not much had changed. It was a beautiful world and it was an ugly world and I was very much in it and part of it. Part of the solution and part of the problem. And all I could do was find my footing again, walk out of that water and stand there on the shore, stunned. I would try to get my bearings, try to re-establish in my head the lay of the land around me and determine which way to walk if I wanted to find my way home.

Year Two

June 20

Potholes and Poetry

L eslie Road is famous for its potholes. The road was named for a former family who lived in these parts, not for me. It is an unpaved gravel road not far from the Atlantic Ocean which arcs through a salt marsh that would swallow the road if it could get away with it. The road silts in with snowdrifts in the winter, making it impassable. In the summer, it dries up and creates great clouds of gritty dust when out-of-town drivers discover its existence. I was once in charge of a small ad hoc, rural committee to prevent the paving of Leslie Road. We won that battle, which I occasionally regret. Well, someone had to stand up to impede progress. I had not only been the spokesperson for that altruistic cause, but I inadvertently saved my government many thousands of dollars that they went on to spend on streetlights for rural areas where street-lights were unwanted.

Potholes form at any time of the year, but late spring and early summer are their favoured season of growth. Here in Nova Scotia, June is like monsoon season in India, but without the malaria. And it's a tad cooler.

I'm sure there is a wonderful lesson in science to be had by the study of the formation of potholes but I'm not that well equipped for the research. As a young man, I had aspirations to be a marine biologist, floating around on big boats like Jacques Cousteau's, with many slender, bikinied assistants. I was alarmed and disheartened, however, to learn that one needed to master many forms of mathematics, including word problems, to be a marine biologist. I bailed out of my marine biology program in university after a dismal semester trying to absorb humourless subjects like calculus and organic chemistry. I opted, instead, for being a poet and threw myself into this coastal wilderness to ply my trade. Thus leaving me to live in an old drafty house on a potholed road, fighting progress with pen and wit as best I could.

But not to cop out entirely, I should, for the uninformed, try to explain the basic nature of potholes. It goes like this:

1. On a dry gravel road that has been "graded" by a large reptilian machine, rain falls. For any number of reasons, small indentations form.

2. Each indentation fills with water from the sky and, when a car tire touches that small indentation, it drives the water out and with it, some of Leslie Road (or any other gravel road it chooses for a home).

3. This happens over and over.

4. The potholes "grow" although they don't really grow at all; they deepen.

5. Then they multiply like tribbles on the Starship *Enterprise*. Walking down a road with a multitude of potholes is really not that bad. One dances around them – or so it seems, if your step is light and if you have any flow to your walking pattern. Viewed from above by a scientist in, say, a helicopter, a very interesting pattern could be established and much could be learned about movement of molecules, string theory, chaos theory, market volatility and the very essence of the universe.

But walking isn't really the problem. Driving is. I write this because right now, Leslie Road is the worst it's ever been when it comes to potholes. The government is refusing to send the road grader until "things dry up." But that will be too late.

In order to get on with my job (as a poet and several other less high-minded endeavours) I must drive a mile or so down Leslie Road and negotiate the potholes. My life is currently filled with negotiations of all sorts involving business deals (the non-poet side of me) and contracts and general people problems that arise.

Facing the mile or so of potholes each morning means that my mind is already engaged in dealing with complex, multilevel problem solving. I am engaged in pothole negotiations as soon as I am out of my driveway and I would argue I am a better man for it.

There is not much traffic on our road – especially when the potholes have blossomed like this. Everyone is trying to avoid the car repair bills that go along with slamming into potholes. I have no real choice so I drive slow and weave intricate paths, often scratching my car on the roses and blackberry thorns by the side of the road or dipping a wheel into the soft pliable shoulder. Some days I succeed in minimizing contact with potholes but as of now, that is almost impossible so I drive through the potholes that are shallow – which, in the long run, will make them deeper.

Potholes never fill back in of their own accord as far as I can tell.

One young guy who lives on our road drives straight down the road pretending the potholes are not there. He has a loud stereo in his car that seals him off from the outside, (so-called) real world and he doesn't give a shit if he's slamming into potholes. He drives. He's no wimp.

I, however, am cautious. Poems do not tend to pay for front-end work. On the economic scale of things, poetry writing is way down there and front-end repair work is way up. So I have to drive slowly.

I try to keep an open mind about everything. I like to look for new options. Spending a lot of time at a desk and before a computer (the old-fashioned kind that poets write on) I seek out escape from indoor work. I need the extra adrenalin or whatever it is produced by physical exercise. A morning wrestling with a faulty metaphor or irrelevant oxymoron sometimes sends me out for a brisk walk in the frigid March wind until I am white-knuckled, teary-eyed, toe-frozen and feeling healthy.

But now it is June and the highway people have told me that pothole repair is perhaps months off because they have used up allocated funding for grader work on my road. At first I feel stymied but then the creative side of my brain, the right hemisphere, has an idea.

I propose this to a guy named Dave at Pothole Repair HQ: "What if you just sent a truck down with some stones, Dave?" I suggest. "You could dump off small piles at intervals along Leslie Road and when I need a break from writing, I will volunteer to go out and fill potholes with my shovel."

Dave laughs. He has never heard such a preposterous thing in his life.

"We couldn't do that," he says, still laughing heartily into the phone receiver.

"I really wouldn't mind. I would do this on regular basis. Maybe every day." I begin to envision this as a great altruistic excuse to get out of the house. In my own way, I would be "avoiding work" by doing something that was not my real job. It would be exercise. It would be productive. "I'm not kidding. I actually think this would be fun."

Dave stops laughing. He is sure he knows a scam artist when he hears one. "If we put piles of stones along roads just anywhere," he suddenly says soberly, "people would steal them and put them on their driveways."

That's what he believes I am up to. He thinks I would be so selfish as to "steal" taxpayers' stones and crushed gravel and use it for my own vile purposes – maybe filling only the potholes in my own driveway.

"I wouldn't do that, Dave. I'm trying to help out."

"I'm sorry, it can't be done."

And that was the end of the phone conversation. I wondered if this was the way Jacques Cousteau was treated when he said he was trying to save the oceans.

Suddenly I became very saddened by the bad turn of events. Deprived of being able to execute my grand plan, I suddenly craved to be out there with a good long-handled shovel, repairing potholes on a mild sunny day. I wanted my neighbours to admire me for my community spirit. I truly wanted to be a pothole repair artist.

Later, I tried one more phone call to Dave's boss, a man who worked downtown in the government office. He'd already been alerted, however, to the possibility of a crank caller wanting to fill potholes out of the supposed goodness of his own heart. The bureaucrat on the end of the line added more negative news. If I filled potholes for free I would be interfering with the jobs of his men who graded roads and filled potholes for a living. There were union issues.

"As soon as citizens start doing road repair on their own, a lot of jobs would be lost, including mine. If I were you, I would not want to steal another man's income." He seemed to miss out on the point that no one was filling the potholes. There was no work being done.

"Sorry," I said finally. "I was only trying to help."

"Well, I would just let it rest if I were you."

But I didn't let it rest. I went out on the road, anyway, and tried fixing a couple of potholes in front of my house. I had a pickaxe and a shovel but no fresh supply of gravel. I discovered the best I could do was turn a small, deep pothole into a wide, shallow pothole that would soon enough become a wide, deep pothole. Here was disappointment again and more information to contemplate about the very complex scheme by which the universe operated. Maybe this was the way I was dealing with problems in my life – turning a small, deep pothole into a wide, deep pothole as I tried to patch things up. Oh, bloody hell.

Despite the fact that we were heading into summer, cold, hard rain was pelting me from a northerly wind and so I retreated inside to read Robert Burton's *The Anatomy of Melancholy*.

But my brain had not let go of this thing. *If*, and it was as always a big if, I were given the chance to convince the highways men to drop off those piles of stones, I would not only fill potholes, but set in motion a new trend. My neighbours, I bet, would follow my lead and help out. Filling potholes would be like a hobby.

No, it would be more than a hobby. Others who didn't even live on the road would come out with shovels and fill potholes because, like me, they truly enjoyed the exercise and the mental satisfaction of levelling and fixing and giving instead of just taking. I was remembering that people actually paid money to go to gyms and fitness centres to do strenuous exercise and this pothole filling thing was certainly much better than that. For free, you could shovel and lift and be outdoors in the fresh air.

Once I worked the media on this idea, I envisioned people driving out from the city with newly purchased shovels to fill potholes on Leslie Road. Once my road was all fixed, they would seek out other rural locations and fill potholes to their heart's content. People would become healthier, lives would be more meaningful. Young men would meet young women while out filling potholes and some would fall in love and get married.

There would be positive economic spin-off as well. Word would leak out; hell, the concept would be grabbed by government tourism promoters and travel entrepreneurs. Europeans would be lured to come here for pothole repair vacations, paying larger sums of money to check in to bed and breakfasts or even pothole resorts on gravel roads.

If things got too far along, those same highwaymen who once filled potholes would have to be retrained instead to dig potholes in order to fill the demand.

But my guess is that it's not just Leslie Road and this neck of the woods where potholes exist. Wherever there is rain and a gravel (or dirt, or mud) road, there would be potholes. Pothole filling, I am sure, could one day become a global activity creating new bonds of peace and understanding. There will be songs about the satisfaction of the pick axe and shovel work. There would be visual art, major motion pictures and many, many books. Deep books. Philosophical books. And poems too. I'm pretty sure there will be pothole poetry.

July 2

Solar Winds in a Random Universe

On the 28th day of June, 4.6 billion years after this planet came into being, there was a photograph on the cover of the *New York Times* showing young men with surfboards on a beach in the Gaza Strip.

I was flying north from New Jersey, home to Nova Scotia, and found the image profoundly moving. It was almost like shouting out to me that the world was going to be okay after all. Generations of violence and hatred would some day end and we would all just go surfing together and share our surfboard wax and our waves.

Surfing is a matter of tapping into energy, riding the wave as it passes beneath you through the ocean. It is quite the little miracle. The Mediterranean Sea, of course, doesn't have waves as powerful as the North Atlantic, mostly for the reason that it is a smaller body of water and bigger waves tend to need more distance to travel.

On my coast we surf both small, local waves and big, hefty waves that have travelled hundreds of miles. Little children on the summer shoreline are fascinated by waves. The water moves in and the water moves out. Sitting on a surfboard, you feel yourself rise, then fall. Waves have high points and low points. Light itself, just for the record, is an electromagnetic wave.

Edwin Schrödinger, an Austrian physicist, was entranced by subatomic particles, the way they behaved and why. He suggested they were bundles of waves and his theory is known as wave mechanics. The year was 1926. He wasn't sure exactly what the waves consisted of. But he could detect the pattern.

On July 2nd, I put my year-old kayak into the water at a place known as Grand Desert. The Acadians who named this place had a sense of humour. There was sand so they called it a desert. There was a big beach so they called it Grand. The water of Chezzetcook Inlet, here near the mouth, is broad and clear and, on this morning, very, very still.

The Canadian military once practised dropping bombs on this beach for a couple of decades, from the fifties into the seventies. When most of the headland had disappeared, from the bombs and from the natural erosion, they gave up and took up video games for practice. Once, years ago, I was sitting on my surfboard not far from the tip of the headland while the Canadian bombers were dumping their cargo. A bomb must have caught on the bomb bay door and not released until the plane was on the ascent beyond the bombing range.

It came down with an impressive splash not far from where I was minding my own business but, lucky for me, it did not go off. Had it exploded, it too would have generated waves of its own as the energy transferred into the seawater, moving out in all directions at once.

A quiet morning in a kayak, at the mouth of an inlet in summer. Alone, paddling very slowly. Red Island ahead. Uninhabited. A few deep rolling swells pass beneath me and I look down into the clear water, able to see the sandy bottom far beneath.

I arrive at the island and beach the kayak in a tiny crescent of sand. It seems as if someone has arranged a garden of driftwood here, chest high – bleached tree stumps with roots still attached, ornate, beautiful. I decide to hike the perimeter of the island and see what there is to discover.

It seems I am permitted on this particular morning to drop out of time. The world goes on without me and I have no purpose except to find what there is to find on my island universe and ponder in my usual way why things are the way they are.

For much of our lives we seek explanations – science does this, as does history and psychology, and religion, of course. But once we have the explanation for a thing, does that make our lives better? I doubt it.

We like our explanations to be logical and comprehendible but that is probably because we pretend to have (or desire to possess) tidy minds. Mine is not a tidy mind, seeking as I am for random connections. Niels Bohr was a Danish physicist. He was one of my childhood heroes, even though I didn't understand his science in the slightest. He once objected to a newly proposed theory in his field because it was "not crazy enough." Bohr, who helped set quantum physics in motion, was hinting at the idea that we lived in a very goofy universe. The old, dull linear notions of science had had their day and should be left behind.

Don't trust me on any of this, please. Remember I am in my island universe today and processing what I believe to be true but may prove to be the ravings of a madman. I have been privileged to paddle a mile or two to a place without people. I hike for a while and sit with my notebook and sometimes books of science and religion and let the mind go. I'm adrift on solar winds in a random universe. If I'm lucky, I will return to my kayak before the incoming tide has risen high up into the driftwood gallery and stolen it away. If that were to happen, though, I would be eating molluscs and orach for dinner, watching gulls and cormorants this evening instead of *Star Trek* reruns. It would not be so bad.

Einstein surmised that light moved through space in the form of "particles," which we later labelled photons. This suggests that those photon torpedoes are severely misnamed. If I had a small flashlight with me, it would suffice as a photon torpedo. If it was dark, and I was trying to keep bats away.

Before Einstein, Max Planck had "proven" that light emitted from matter was shot out in bursts or packets of energy he called quanta. As this all headed into quantum mechanics, the evidence kept appearing that light is both wave energy and particles at the same time. This would be crazy enough to satisfy Niels Bohr.

Crazy enough to satisfy me.

Better yet, attempts to track down the subatomic particles indicated that they could be in two places at the same time. Oh, really?

And if subatomic particles can do that, why can't we?

If subatomic particles are both matter and energy, that's how they do it, my guess would be. But I myself am both matter and energy – bundles of energy, in fact. And if motivated, I will work on being at two places at one time, I promise.

But it is difficult enough to be one place at one time. I'm forever hard at work (and failing) at the old practice of trying to be here and now. Red Island, mid-inlet, summer morning. I am also walking on that beach in the Gaza Strip, my surfboard under my arm. Palestinians and Israeli surfers left and right of me wearing the same sun block on their noses. Zinc shields. One loans the other some of his wax. Armageddon cancelled because of small but good waves out on the sandbar.

It may have been Stephen Hawking who suggested that before the universe began, time did not exist. My mother said this to me back when I was quite young and we were headed to a dentist appointment. I was maybe eight and I wanted to stay home and watch the end of the Bugs Bunny cartoon show but my mother said, flat out, "There is no time."

She probably didn't mean it the way Hawking did but there it is, the phrase from childhood. Time may not exist except in the eye of the beholder. But I digress.

I pause at a small beach and note the edible wild plants: orach, pigweed, sea rocket, glasswort (one of my faves), sea oats and beach peas. There are viny things that I've never been able to label. Everything arranged in perfect order or arranged randomly, depending on how you want to look at it. I drink water from my bottle and look up at the morning sun, remembering that it was a good five billion years ago that the solar system started to "condense." In those days, all the matter on this beach and everywhere else in the solar system was just dust and gas – not very glamorous origins, for sure. Good thing gravity was on our side to sort it all out.

In the early days of the earth, it was bombarded by asteroids which helped to give the planet more mass, a kind of bulking up for the big game: life on earth. The earth pretty much invented itself – at least that's the way I want to look at it on this morning and it is *my* morning. I get to make my own rules. I ponder science when I want to, look at bugs and razor clams when I see fit. I have invented my own version of time and my own rules.

And how exactly did the earth invent oxygen? You may wonder this if you happen to be a sparrow clinging to an arced stalk of sea oats in my small island audience.

The answer, and this will be on the test, is bacteria. I won't go into the complexities because I don't know enough science but it *was* bacteria. Took one thing and turned it into another. In this case we got pure oxygen so creatures to follow could breathe, if they wanted to.

Crazy as it sounds to the layperson, but right down Niels Bohr's attitude alley. There it is. And how many holidays do you suppose humans have established to pay homage to bacteria? You do the math.

I walk on, continuing with my perimeter path until I arrive at a long sweeping beach facing south, towards the open ocean. On first sight, there is nothing here. Until I sit down and discover the beach is a virtual megalopolis of some kind of hopping shrimp-like creatures. They burrow holes in the sand, pushing it out of the hole with their rear legs. Some crawl, some wander, some leap like pole-vaulters three feet at a time. Some are fighting – they have not heard about the Gaza Strip and that peace is breaking out in all the corners of the world. I break up the fight as gently as I can and move the two pugilists to opposite ends of the beach, wondering what they think has just happened. What explanation could be possible to put forward when they each go home to the burrow at night to explain to the wife.

Face down on the sand I continue to watch the bug frenzy. Digging, jumping, collecting food from beneath the sand. Front leaps, back flips. It's a pretty good show.

But the tide is rising. If Shakyamuni Buddha were here with me (and he probably is in one form or another) he would have no problem making the connection between the gymnastic beach shrimp and the kindly ancestral bacteria and the whole business of being both matter and energy at the same time. Everything is changing, everything is the same, he might remind me. I remind myself of this as we walk together toward my end and starting point on the other side of the island, wanting full circle, trusting my kayak to still be there.

My nearly-tangible Buddha – still portly and happy, robed and sandalled – has gently bullied physics aside for the nonce to remind me of his concern over suffering. The whole idea of suffering is such a "modern" notion, he reminds me. Was anything suffering twelve billion years ago, or 4.6 million for that matter or back when the bacteria were busy with oxygen ambitions? I think not.

Suffering, Buddha reminds me, is created by the human mind. The mind is a wonderful invention, no doubt about it. It created ice cream and 1957 Chevy station wagons and even compassion. But it also has created a big whack of human grief.

Ordinary suffering is when you don't get something you want. Unhappiness is also caused by change. Good stuff is happening to you and then it stops. (It's not fair, is it? your mind asks.) Attached to that is the fact that *nothing* ever stays the same. All the great poets moaned poetically about this so-called "mutability" of things.

This grand philosophic morning will not last and soon I will be sitting in a tiresome meeting discussing God knows what trivial thing. We wish to hold onto the moments we like and so we etch them in our memory or we buy digital cameras. But it is never ever enough.

There are deer tracks on the sand now and the footprint of another creature I do not recognize – a cookie cutter kind of track, possibly a bobcat. Animals may have found their way here from the north, over frozen ice in the winter. If so, what would have prompted the rather long and dangerous adventure?

Buddha has slipped off and away as the wind begins to rise and, distracted by the sound of orchestral sparrows and goldfinches in the trees, I trip on an exposed root and fall on a rock. My knee connects hard, this big bony English knee I inherited from my great-great-grandfather, William Percival Choyce. There is pain and, some suffering, but then it is temporary as are all things and, if I have it right, the actual suffering part here was not caused by me or the root or the bird's song but the suffering comes from inside; it is caused by me.

I am reminded of the story of the Zen master with the somewhat naive student. The Zen master, not paying great attention to where he was sitting down, one day sat down on a needle. He yelped, "Ouch," or something more offensive in front of his young student. The student seeing this reaction lost all faith, assuming that if the master was truly enlightened he would not have felt the pain. As the student set off into the world to find another teacher, the Zen master was disappointed that he had not instilled in his student the truth that neither the needle, nor the master, nor the sound that issued from his mouth really existed.

We westerners, even an east coast westerner like me, always have problems with the being/non-being business. It seems like we should be one or the other. But Niels Bohr would be satisfied that it's "crazy" enough that we both exist and don't exist at the same time. From one point of view I am only matter, a limping guy on a shoreline rounding a headland. From another, I am a translation of energy, a pulse, a wave travelling distance and time. From another point of view, I am neither.

The distant headland of East Chezzetcook appears to my eye to be an island, unattached to the mainland. This seems impossible since I was there a year ago and I could walk to the fish shacks out there. From here it appears adrift and I am disoriented by this notion, naturally wondering if my mental gymnastics have tripped me into any of the possible alternate universes.

Ahead is a big wooden crate, a box four feet by four feet by four feet, set at the high tide mark. It is something that must have fallen from a trawler, perhaps. There is water inside and an amazing aquarium of life: periwinkles, snails, mussels, scarves of algae and moss above the water line. A few tiny fish and even a pair of starfish. It is an odd little universe unto itself, a box that nothing inside could possibly leave unless a monster squall filled it to the brim with rain.

I jump to the conclusion that the creatures inside are unaware that there is another larger world around them. Everything appears to be quite healthy down there in the box. The snails are crawling ever so slowly. The barnacles don't seem at all despondent. The algae is blooming. From my perspective, they are all trapped but what do I know? I think I am freely wandering around an island in the North Atlantic pondering Buddha and physics and being entertained by broad-jumping shrimp. As far as these things go, the crowd down in the fish crate might be a saltwater utopia.

Actually, I guess I've been trying to claw my way out of my box for years, sometimes with grand results, sometimes with yelps of pain. Sometimes, I give up even thinking about it, cynically expecting that, once free of one box, I'd discover I am only in a somewhat larger, probably more dangerous, box and there is a larger one beyond that.

someday maybe if I married Miss America, we would be helping to unite the two kinds of people in the world. "And that would be a good thing, right?" I asked Minnie.

Minnie was playing solitaire as I watched. I thought she was old and clever. Old meant fifty or so then, I guess. Clever meant she had a good vocabulary and spoke fast. Minnie had an answer for anything I asked and if she didn't she'd haul out a dictionary or a single volume encyclopaedia and look it up. She didn't give a rat's ass if the answer was found in a book that was over thirty years old. Minnie's answer to my question did not require a book. She said simply, "Marriage isn't always the way it appears in the movies."

This was to imply that her marriage wasn't always an easy one. The married people in movies she was referring to were probably Jimmy Stewart and Donna Reid. She was married to Avery Willis, still known to his grandchildren as Gaga. Even Minnie had started calling him Gaga. Gaga was in the next room lying on the couch, the chesterfield as he called it, watching *Gunsmoke* on TV. Gaga wished he'd been a cowboy instead of a farmer but he had his prize yellow Burpee corn to grow and he was doing all right when he wasn't wrestling with big coils of lima bean wire or filling out income tax forms.

Gaga was English, I suppose. He claimed that his ancestors came from England with Lord Baltimore in the eighteenth century. This was the same Lord Baltimore who took a hand in settling Newfoundland, I think, but found it too inhospitable and went south to create Maryland. The Willises spread out around Chesapeake Bay and that's where Avery had grown up, on the Eastern Shore of Maryland. According to Gaga, the Eastern Shore of Maryland was oyster heaven. If it wasn't for World War One he might have stayed there. Even though Gaga got sick in France and nearly died, he remembers everything about his part in the Great War as the best time of his life. Gaga would sometimes tell me, "There will be another great war soon, just wait and see." He said this any time Nikita Khrushchev was shown on the nightly news.

Gaga was trying to sound wise like Minnie but it wasn't the same kind of gum-clicking wisdom. Gaga's wisdom came from a deep-seated cynicism that was like the phlegm he would haul up out of his throat out in the field to spit into the dry soil.

Gaga believed we would go to war with the Russians sooner or later, and he figured we could whip them. On TV, he'd seen Khrushchev bang his shoe on his desk at the UN and figured all the Russians were angry like that. My grandfather may have even thought war was a potentially good thing. He wasn't thinking of nuclear devastation because that was still so unthinkable. But then, the devastation of the First World War had been unimaginable as well. Gaga openly professed that the darn Russians deserved whatever we threw at them. But he wasn't going to convince me.

My grandfather was not without prejudice. His views on race were pre-twentieth century and southern. He was civil to virtually any person of colour he encountered but in private he would offer up his opinions about a person based on their ethnic background. It was like someone had imprinted a template in his brain when he was very young. Black people are this. Italians this. The French had been kind to him while he was convalescing in a hospital in Brittany but because they did not speak English, he believed they were lesser mortals.

Of course, he had opinions about other white people too. He made broad strokes with his pen of opinion and corralled people into categories according to where they lived or what their occupation was. All lawyers were thieves. All teachers thought they were smarter than they really were. Anyone who lived in New York City was a fool. People who lived in Pennsylvania – well, he couldn't understand why anyone lived in Pennsylvania since he felt things were so much better where we lived in New Jersey. But that was because we lived in South Jersey, not North Jersey.

He had no opinions about Canadians whatsoever. He'd never really thought about Canada. Years later when I told him I was moving to Canada, he didn't know what to make of it. People around him were moving to California or Florida or Texas. But Canada? I explained I was moving to Nova Scotia, near Halifax.

"Halifax," he said, something finally registering. "Back during the war, when we wanted to say Hell but were in polite company, we would always say Halifax."

Bombs were exploding in trenches, mustard gas canisters were going off, deploying their toxic gases presumably and if polite company were nearby someone would yell, "Let's get the Halifax out of here!"

Or if you politely wanted to tell someone to go to hell, you told him or her to vacate to the provincial capital of this eastern Canadian province.

Gaga held the English in high regard but admitted that they had degenerated some since the departure of Lord Baltimore and his émigrés.

Often in the mid-sixties, if I were sitting with my grandfather in his living room and he was educating me on the nature of human nature, my grandmother would charge into the room – because Minnie charged everywhere, she did not walk or breeze or sally – and begin playing her baby grand piano. She would play the bicycle built for two song and her voice would warble. She sang loudly and drowned out all of her husband's opinions and she seemed to do it on purpose. And he seemed not to mind.

Minnie's ancestors too were English. Her father's last name was "Dumble" and I was often thankful that I had not ended up with Dumble for a last name. It was a Dickensian name worthy of humour but Minnie never complained of any problems with it. Maybe it's because Minnie had several powerful credos that she had developed for herself. One of her favourites was the expression, "Life should be spent, not saved," which I would later learn came from none other than D.H. Lawrence. It seems inconceivable to me that Minnie had read Lawrence but then she was full of surprises. She was the only person, for example, I had ever met in my entire lifetime who had actually read *The Last of the Mohicans* without being forced to do so in school. James Fennimore Cooper was a very famous dead New Jersey writer that no one ever read unless they were forced to. People visited the famous South Jersey home of Cooper but none dared to read his books.

About the Lawrence quote, though, I have a feeling that it was something he himself had borrowed along the way of his writing career. Writers do that. They pick up things not previously written down and call them their own. My own opinion is that the Dumbles were English as were the Lawrences and that somewhere in English history family paths crossed and the expression actually found its way to the Lawrences from the Dumbles.

The Willises and Dumbles are on my mother's side. I don't think my mother ever saw herself as anything but American nor did my father. And I sincerely doubt that it ever once occurred to them that they would have a son who would grow up and become a Canadian, let alone a Nova Scotian. And just for the record, if I had to choose priority, I would say I am a Nova Scotian first and a Canadian second. If Nova Scotia seceded and became part of Iceland, then I would become an Icelander. It's not that I am in any way anti-Canadian. I am just loyal to the soil I live on here by the sea.

With that off my chest, I move on to an analysis of my father's side of the family. My father would be nearly in his fifties before a distant relative would heat up the family interest in genealogy. It turns out there was a Richard Choyce who moved from England to New Jersey in the eighteenth century. He had a big family and the Choyces descended into the fields and valleys of New Jersey and eastern Pennsylvania. By the time the middle of the twentieth century rolled around, some of the Choyce men were plumbers, some drove bread and milk trucks, one sold aluminium siding, another used cars. My father was a milk truck mechanic.

The Choyce family tree had its roots in Leicester, England, cousin Betty discovered. She was tracking down Choyces all around the world, including the other Leslie Choyce who had lived in Nova Scotia and later Montreal and died the very same year I moved to Canada – as if this nation was not large enough to accommodate two Les Choyces.

Well, I was always pretty disappointed to learn we had virtually nothing of what I considered real ethnic background in the Choyce clan. We were just dull white American people descended from some dull, dead English white people of Leicester, England. Like other immigrant English families, I'm sure we wreaked havoc on the New World with our smug opinions and English ways of having our way. For all that, I apologize, although it probably doesn't do a Halifax lot of good.

Not long after I moved to Canada, I received a letter from an ad hoc historical committee in Flemington, New Jersey. They were looking for money from me to help save a small dilapidated cemetery near Flemington that was about to be ploughed under and turned into a parking lot for a K Mart store. Some dead Choyces were buried there and the ad hoc committee was convinced I'd be incensed about this desecration of my ancestors. Richard Percival Choyce himself was buried there – my great-great-great grandfather.

I tried to muster up some furore over this despicable lack of regard for the dead but failed to come up with more than twenty dollars (Canadian) to go towards the legal defence. I could see that this kind of legal battle would be a real cash cow for North Jersey lawyers and I wasn't anxious to be embroiled in such a struggle. I'd rather save the whales, the seals, and the diminishing marmots of Vancouver Island. The cemetery preservation society took my money but I never heard back from them. I assume that progress rolled all over that little sad cemetery and by now the K Mart has probably been abandoned and will be torn down in favour of a new Staples store or Toys "R" Us.

On my father's mother's side, there turned out to be some small hope for ethnicity, at long last. She was born a Bauer and, for some reason, she had thought there was Welsh blood in her and so in me. I approved of having Welsh blood even though Wales is painfully close to England. But at least there was something Celtic, something a bit Dylan Thomasish. When I learned of my possible Welsh heritage, I began telling people that I was, in fact, Welsh. Later my grandmother revealed the obvious, that her family was probably a combination of English and German.

The German influence explained why her potato salad and sauerkraut were so good but it was no comfort to me. While I was more liberal in my attitudes toward the Germans than my grandfather, Gaga, I knew the blundering Germans had done as much harm – or more – historically to the world as the English.

I am still hoping that there is a tad of Welsh in me all these many years later but feel above having too much pride in anything other than the fact that I am a small citizen in a small community somewhere on the northeastern coast of North America. I'm a husband, a father, a writer and a surfer, a friend to animals and sometimes people and, as often as I can, a nice guy to all and sundry, blundering forward like my ancestors but attempting to leave the least amount of destruction possible in my wake. And I promise to take all my trash with me when I leave the forest.

July 12

Twelve Billion Years Old

I wake on a foggy morning twelve billion years into the life cycle of the universe. For all I know, today, July 12th, is the birthday of the universe and therein lies the cause of my celebration.

The experts, the ones who have what they think is evidence, argue about the exact age of the universe. Some say it is as young as ten billion while others think it is as antiquated as fifteen billion. The consensus is twelve.

I do the usual. Get up, eat some breakfast and walk the dog on the beach. It was about a year ago that Jody was as close to death as a dog can get. But today she is fine thanks to her family's loyalty, tenacity, vigilance, medicine, healing thoughts and that colour photo of the old Pope placed beside her.

And today the universe itself is fine. Foggy, but fine. There may be surfable waves by afternoon and the fog may lift. Or not. But I'm on the optimistic side of things today after several dark days brought on by I know not what.

On the beach, the usual miracles. Sand – one of the great inventions of a twelve-billion-year-old universe. Wet stones, each one a collaborator in the eight in the morning artwork of this place. Seaweed, dollops of it, bright rusty threads of it, pulpy shiny glands of it, fine thin slimy sheets of it. All of it asleep, waiting for high tide after a night of sleeping off a great party on the beach.

A blue toy sand shovel: evidence of sun and children in the recent past. And then this, my anchor for the morning. Someone has carried a large flat stone to the wooden walkway and written on it with purple paint, "Nakita, 2003, Indian Brook."

It's been many years now since NASA launched that probe into deep space. Unmanned but full of math and symbols and music and art and a recording of voices, I think. The earth was already filled with silly monuments in arctic and sub-arctic and tropical places, great chunks of granite set down in cities and countrysides to commemorate atrocities and man's predisposition to killing each other. Something more ambitious was in order – a benign bullet shot into the vast emptiness of this small galaxy. (There are so many galaxies and ours is a trifling bit of fluff, or at most, just another face in a vast crowd).

But we do tend to want to leave some evidence that we were here. As Nakita did.

Why the rock is so instructive and pleasing to me I am not sure. But I think it goes like this. I'm fairly sure Nakita is a girl or a young woman – the purple paint, the shape of the well-formed letters. It is an unlikely name for these parts and it reminds of Nikita Khrushchev who has always interested me.

My take on history is that the only reason we are all still alive is that Khrushchev had the good humanitarian sense to back off in 1962 as his USSR naval men were hauling missiles to Cuba. John F. Kennedy threatened all-out nuclear war if he didn't stop the shipment. The US already had nuclear missiles not far from the Soviet border in Turkey and Khrushchev had hoped to balance things but Kennedy would have none of it.

In those days, I was but a boy and practising for nuclear attacks at school by going into the hallway and kneeling with my head down facing the wall. Teachers would scold you if you poked your head up, admonishing that if you popped your head up, you would get radiation in your eyes and go blind.

I knew enough science even then to realize that, head up or head down, if we were anywhere near a nuclear blast, we were going to be smoke. It wasn't like we would be able to get up after it was all over, brush off the dust and go home to dinner.

Like everyone else in my school, I thought we were the good guys and thought Kennedy was a pretty sharp president. But it wasn't until nearly two decades later that I realized Nikita Khrushchev was the one man who saved us from global calamity on that fateful day.

As I write this, I drift off to look at a small plastic globe sitting in my window. The sun fades the colours of nations. Canada is a large northern faint-pink country. Mexico is a pale yellow place and the United States, once the sun has altered a prominent green country to light blue, is the same colour as the Atlantic and Pacific Oceans. The effect is startling. It is as if it is not there. Canada hovers like a great craggy island at the top of the world and Mexico has a northerly coastline. There appears to be an easy navigational path between England and Japan.

Nova Scotia looks like a small narrow appendage dangling from what's left of the continent.

The seas will reshape all of our native lands any way it damn well wants to when the time comes. My beach is being consumed by the Atlantic and may be gone within my lifetime, so I'm committed to walking it each morning to get my money's worth out of it before it goes.

I should also point out that Nakita's rock noted the year, 2003. Not the exact date, just the year. She clearly had some expectation that people will be noticing that rock, saying to themselves, Nakita was here in the year 2003. Imagine that. She will be old and wise and charming by then. I know this to be true.

The fact she is from the small inland community of Indian Brook assures me that she is in fact Mi'kmaq – descended from the first people who lived in Nova Scotia. The Mi'kmaq have been living here for about 12,000 years, if we are interpreting the evidence correctly. My own ancestors, the Europeans, have been here less than five hundred years. We are not as good at sharing the wealth of this place as the Mi'kmaq have been.

The beach, Lawrencetown, named for the military governor responsible for the expulsion of the Acadians and atrocities against the Mi'kmaq, was a place where the Mi'kmaq people would migrate to in the summer. It was a place of great bounty – fish and clams and mussels and more. But in the winter, the Mi'kmaq wisely retreated to the inland forests, following waterways north into the interior.

I don't ever see many Mi'kmaq people on the beach on hot summer days when the thin strip of sand is crowded with pale city people stretched out on towels, looking oiled and bored.

As you may recall, the earth has existed for 4.6 billion years. It took 7.4 billion years before that for the expanding universe to contrive a planet where people would one day invent computers, chewing gum and surfboards. But it was in the schematic from the beginning.

Our spinning sphere was a ball of boiling goo until 3.8 billion years back, at which point some hard surfaces appeared and oceans were in the works. Evidence of life is dated as far back as 3.5 billion years, which, if you think about it, suggests that it came on the scene fairly quickly. This life took the form of blue-green algae not much different from that in the ponds in the salt marsh beyond my garden.

I used to buy the family some fairly expensive supplements of dried blue-green algae that came from a lake in Oregon. It may have done some good and we only quit taking it because it was so darn expensive. This is odd, of course, realizing that it is a form of life that's been around for 3.5 billion years and such a common commodity in the world. Some people think of blue-green algae as not much more than pond scum. But just because it can't play chess, it doesn't mean it is less important than you or me. Far from it.

On the week leading up to this birthday of the universe, this foggy Saturday commemorating that extraordinary explosion that set everything in motion, I gave myself (being an intrinsic part of the universe) a series of presents.

One was a journey to a remote Bay of Fundy stretch of shoreline that I'll call Crystal Cliffs. Crystal because there is amethyst to be found there. Cliffs because you have to lower yourself down to sea level by an extraordinary series of ropes. My friend Lou went with me, each of us uncertain about finding the right path through the dense spruce forest or if we could hoist ourselves back up the cliffs once we made it down.

Lou is a psychologist by profession and he and I hike to remote places to get away from civilization as much as is humanly possible in this century. I don't think he shared my enthusiasm for the upcoming birthday of the universe and wasn't convinced that I knew exactly which day it was. But I tried to explain it was like other shifty holidays: Easter or Christmas, for that matter. Washington's Birthday, even, was sometimes shifted around by the wily Americans to allow for long weekends, wasn't it?

In order to get to our destination we drove to the Fundy Shore and parked at the very end of the road. The great thing about this shoreline is that this is where two continents collided and pulled apart millions of years ago. What was once the landmass of Gondwana had wandered north and west and smashed right into what was the old version of North America. It was a slow crash by modern standards but monumental. It shoved rock that was once horizontal into vertical formations, and it brought to the surface quite a bit of unusual rock that was usually found deep below the surface.

Fortunately, it was not the sort of collision where lawyers were involved because there were no people around. Mostly just rocks, who had the run of things in those days.

Gondwana eventually became tired of being jammed up against old North America, grew restless in a geological sort of way and headed off south and east to become, *ta da*, Africa. However, a fairly large chunk was left over, like a scrap of somebody's fender stuck to your bumper after a car crash. That fender became much of Nova Scotia, dangling out in the Atlantic shaped like a lobster.

So Lou and I were at the crash site. The trail to the cliffs was not obvious and a local woman pretended she didn't know the route. This made perfectly good sense because, once we made it to the rope drop, we realized it was a perfect place for the average person to fall several hundred feet onto old Gondwana rocks.

She said, though, we could talk to her uncle, Carl. Carl was stacking firewood in the neatest configuration I had ever seen. It was summer and the need for the wood was a long way off but Carl's stacking had a kind of geometric precision. I asked about the path to the cliffs and I could tell he was sizing me up.

I had a one-strapped European backpack that had the logo for a French party drink. This did not speak of cliff climbing expertise. I could see the doubt in his face. But he looked at my shoes and then back at his firewood. He took a deep breath and then gazed across his pasture.

"There," he said. "Walk across the field until you see the path by those blown-down trees. Go to the top of the ridge and veer to the right, then go left if you can find the path going down."

Lou and I had several debates as to which was the right path or if we were even on a path. We stuck to the basic theory of going up and then down for we knew we had to cross a ridge. We veered at what we thought was a good place to veer and then explored several dead ends until we found a path that led to the ropes.

The ropes were a series of various old fishing ropes tied to trees and roots that were amazingly cemented to the side of this very steep piece of real estate. The footing was loose gravel or crumbly rock. The descent was breathtaking.

Once we dropped to sea level, we had arrived at the proverbial land that time forgot. High rock cliffs to the north, wide stony plain to the south – low tide on the Bay of Fundy. Not a soul in sight. No boats, no houses, nothing. Just us. Two boys with rucksacks looking for rocks.

The tides of the Bay of Fundy are legendary in that they drop so far and sweep back in so quickly. The tourism departments of New Brunswick and Nova Scotia speak of them as being the "highest tides in the world." Because Fundy is a funnel, it has an amazing capacity to drain itself quite low and then as the tide comes back in, it compresses a massive amount of water into an ever more narrow space until you get a tidal bore sweeping up the smaller tributaries. In full surge, it is said that the volume of the flow of the water in the Bay of Fundy is equivalent to the "output of all the world's combined rivers." How someone figured that out is beyond my comprehension as many things are. But it could draw more tourists if promoted on the Internet, I am sure.

One of my dreams is to surf the front of the tidal bore, muddy as it is, but I've tried and failed twice, getting dragged a mile or so until beaching myself on a sandbar (mudbar, really).

Today we had about two hours of low tide before the flow would reverse itself and come washing back in. We had been warned that if we did not retreat up the ropes soon enough after the tide's turning, we could be in big trouble. If we were a mile or so away, with sheer rock cliffs to our backs, there would be no way out. People had drowned here. Others had been rescued by Sea King helicopters.

I claimed that I wasn't worried. Lou was more respectful of things neither of us understood, a good tactic for a psychologist hiking with a half-crazed poet blathering on about the age of the universe. Lou wondered out loud exactly where all that water went, when the tide when out.

"It goes back into the sea," I suggested.

"But we live by the sea on the other side of the province," he reminded me. "And the tide goes out there too.

"Maybe it goes to Europe," I suggested.

"Or the other side of the planet."

"I know it has something to do with the moon," I offered up.

Lou shrugged. We had not a clue as to where the water went when the tide went out. Between us we had four graduate degrees and not one solid clue about where water went at low tide or why it bothered returning to our shoreline at the appropriate time. It was a dazzling failure of the North American education system and we were both impressed by the poverty of our knowledge.

Not entirely clueless when it came to the age of the universe or the history of the geology at hand, I knew that geologists had been here before. Two codgers named Alger and Jackson had been poking around near here in the 1820s. Jackson, the more poetic of the two, wrote, "The visitor, in addition to the wildness and picturesque beauty of the scene, will find the field so richly stocked with minerals that he will delight to linger on the spot and gather these objects of science."

I envisioned Lou and me hefting heavy payloads of amethyst – the currently desired gem of the day – up those nearly dependable dangling ropes.

We walked the rocky shoreline for a bit until we came to a likely place to search for rare rocks: a chunk of fallen cliff face. We knew that geodes, agates and even amethyst could be found inside seemingly dull, uninspiring rocks. And there were many dull uninspiring rocks. Lou had a hammer and chisel, which surprised me that he had come so well prepared. I myself was expecting amethyst to jump out at me and command my attention.

My own research had led me to understand that much of the ordinary uninspiring rock was basalt but there was also Triassic red sandstone and shale, even some Triassic limestone. I tossed the word Triassic around quite a bit while poking away at the cliff face with my bare hands, disturbing millennia of the hard earth-building work that had situated the rocks here. The basalt had come from lava; that would be your igneous rock, left over from back when the planet was cooling. Now we were at least getting ourselves back into the past, closer by a breath at least to the origin of the universe.

Sir William Dawson, back in his 1891 volume *Acadian Geology*, wrote, "The trap formation of Nova Scotia has become somewhat celebrated for the abundance and fineness of the specimens for which it affords." Trap was another word for basalt. I liked the way Dawson spoke of "abundance and fineness," words that one would like to apply to every day of one's life, not just concerning rocks but other pleasures as well.

We wandered off from each other and, from a distance, I listened to the echo of Lou chipping away at the dull rocks looking for gems. I had a small assortment of interesting specimens, none agate, but a geode (a nifty little cave of crystals) nearly as big as a penny and some black dangerous-looking crystal rock that looked like it came from an asteroid.

Sitting on a big boulder eating a sandwich, I saw the tide reverse itself and begin to advance with great rapidity. The amethyst continued to ignore my presence and I hiked back to where Lou was still attempting to bring down a precarious overhang of basalt on his well-educated head.

For our trouble, we had found rocks with names like haematite, gelignite, schist (an old favourite rock name from my youth), dodecahedron magnetite and some prized zeolites that looked like frozen waterfalls of crystal. As the tide advanced, we retreated to the ropes and the rock face for ascent. In truth, my best find of the day was a pinkish white zeolite the size of a beer bottle that I picked up randomly right before heading up the ropes. It was strategically placed dull-side up but, once turned over, had a magnificent appearance.

Though I gloated momentarily over my good luck, Lou brought me down out of my glory by pointing out it was unlike any other rock beneath our feet. Some other rock hound had carried it this far but rejected it as too heavy, too unworthy of lugging it up the several hundred feet to the ridge above.

The climb back up the cliffs was straight out of a Harrison Ford adventure movie. The Tim Hortons coffee on the way home tasted better than any cup of coffee produced since the Triassic period.

On the road back to Lawrencetown Beach, to home, I reminded Lou that for the first three billion years on earth, life only existed in the oceans. "And probably for good reason," he said.

"There were no living organisms on land until a mere 400 million years ago," I stated with self-satisfaction. I wanted to go on but Lou was losing interest so my diatribe became internal. And so the tides kept flowing in and out, day after day. Tides always seem to know what they are doing. As do planets in general and galaxies.

There are, they say, no goals of evolution. Shit happens. Purpose or not. Random consequence or divine plan. What humans are referred to – genus Homo – have been on this planet for only two million years. We are a kind of test case for who knows what. We are not particularly adaptable, the biologists would point out. The cockroach, for example, evolved into its present form 300 million years ago. It can survive almost anywhere on earth on its own without Game Boys, Gore-Tex or SpaghettiOs.

Today, on this warm foggy morning by the sea, I drink in the damp sweet salt air with every pore of my body. I smell the richness of the seawater and the life contained therein. By afternoon there will be waves and I will tap the energy produced by storms hundreds of miles from here as the tide drops a billion gallons of water to go someplace else to an undesignated location.

Nakita's stone anchors me to the present, which is a thing hard enough to do during any one of the twelve billion years this story has been in progress. At fifty-two years old, I have been part of the narrative for only .0000000043 or .043 billionth of a percentage point of the current universal life span. I suppose that makes me sound like a pretty small player in the scheme of things but, for whatever reasons, I am convinced that I am not without significance.

July 27

Orange

The death of my daughters' grandmother takes me to New Jersey where the family is surprised to see me. I am there, of course, to show support. It is the obvious and important thing to do. Relatives and family friends from the past have gathered together. I bring myself and my daughter Sunyata, and I bring Nova Scotia with me. It is important that we all show up for the memorial service.

There is a wonderful upbeat eulogy at the church and then the rest of the event is usurped by religion. I haven't sung "The Old Rugged Cross" or "How Great Thou Art" since I was a teenager so these and other hymnal favourites are like a K-Tel greatest hits CD. I am moved by some of it, amused by some of the archaic language of the lyrics and sing along even though I know I am off-key. I recall that this was one of the things you could get away with in church without people giving you a dirty look.

Two preachers, one a fundamentalist son, Donald, take over with sermons and it seems like one long advertisement for Christianity. Jesus is still superstar and the rules of being one of his groupies even now seem odd to me. I do envy people who can believe that it is possible to die and rise up into a glorious heaven where God appears smiling and hugs you to his bosom. Then in you go and all is happy ever after.

But what exactly do you do there?

If we create our own afterlives out of our beliefs, then I trust that this kind woman, who has died, is there now and all is well as the preaching sales team claims.

No one talks of hell, the other realm situated below to accommodate those excluded from heaven. I'm not sure what has happened to purgatory in modern Christianity, which has opted for a cleaner duality: you are either in or you ain't. But if you are not a true believer, you go to hell. I suppose you go there even if you have doubts. And, of course, you go there if you are not saved.

All my life I have been trying to save myself. I don't think I have ever fully given myself over to a set of beliefs – religious, political or otherwise. I'm of the bootstrap variety, stuck with pulling myself up out of my own weakness and despair. Only lately, in the past few years, teetering along the slippery precipice of depression, have I been able to stick my arm out when I fear falling and ask for help from a few close friends.

So I'm saved for now. But not for good.

On my way back home to Canada, I arrive at the Philadelphia airport at 4:30 in the morning. My father and I drove the empty I95 freeway south, past the dockyard where I saw a considerable portion of the American Naval fleet left over from World War II, past the big stadiums named for ever-changing banks. At the airport, I stand in one line, then another. I pass inspection by security guards who want to look at my shoes and take a chemical swab of the inside of my carry-on bag and test me in other ways.

In Montreal where I make my connection, I stand in three more lines. This is what we do here in the new century. We line up and wait. There is less hired help up front at all the counters so the lines are longer. The airlines are going, or already are, bankrupt but the planes still fly. I see an Air Canada employee, one of those wonderful Quebec women of grace, dignity and generosity. She was very helpful to me once, here at the Dorval airport. I was jet-lagged beyond my limit, travelling home from Europe and having connection problems, and she went out of her way to fix things up.

The airport today is overcrowded and I am actually standing in a line which is the line-up at a far corner of the airport – a line-up to get into the primary line that already crowds the front concourse. When I call to her, she thinks I am just another irate customer wondering what is taking so long. I actually take a chance on leaving my place in the line to walk over to her and say I remember her and thank her for helping me.

She doesn't understand at first. I don't want anything from her. Just saying thanks. She doesn't remember me of course. I'm no movie star, no hockey great. I explain how grateful I was and eventually get a smidge of a smile. She's surprised. In a world of whiners and complainers, there's one guy half-shaved with a mop of uncut hair and coffee stains on his shirt, trying to say something nice to her. She gets it, has only a split second to give me eye contact and nods; then she's off to the far reaches of the airport for those waiting to get in line, to quell some kind of conflict.

When I finally reach the counter, another attendant assigns me seat 1C, executive class, for the final leg of my flight home to Nova Scotia. Sitting in first class is like being in a foreign country. It is not exciting but I have no seatmate and get to curl up in the big seat by the window and read my book, *Paris, 1919*. Lloyd George, Georges Clemenceau and Woodrow Wilson are trying to tidy up the War to End all Wars. They are doing the best they can but it's a real rat's nest – not just Europe, but the world. Wilson is pushing a brilliant but doomed scheme to start the League of Nations, which would be able to sort out each successive crisis as it emerges and enforce a world peace. His health is failing but he will get some semblance of a world organization for peace. Unfortunately, it will not last.

The United States, or at least its conservative politicians, refuses to join. Ultimately, the League fails and there are Nazis and other fascists and small nations wanting to dominate other nations. And there are body parts again of young men from many countries strewn all over farmers' fields and on cobblestoned streets throughout Europe. My father is sent to England to keep the trucks running that supply the bombers and later he is sent to Paris where he meets up with his brothers and then on down to Casablanca, still fixing trucks for the world war that Woodrow Wilson could not stop.

When the Nazis give up, my father goes home on a troop ship and gets ready to go fix some more trucks in the South Pacific where the Pacific war still continues.

The dropping of two nuclear bombs on Hiroshima and Nagasaki changes his travel plans. He can stay at home and return to being a civilian. As a result of that, he marries my mother. They have a first son, Gordy and then me three years later.

If the League of Nations had not failed, I may never have been born. If Harry Truman had not made the decision to drop those nuclear bombs, I most certainly would not have come into this world – at least not as the person I am. Everything would have been different.

It's foggy when I arrive back at Lawrencetown Beach. In my garden by the marsh, there is a surfeit of peas. We eat them raw in my family. The Swiss chard has great ambition with leaves the size of palm fronds. Last year's parsley that has wintered over has gone to seed but the lettuce has a promising career ahead of it and the Egyptian onions are bowed over, as if praying, from the weight of the fruit at their tips.

The yellow and orange calendula flowers, self-seeded and determined to rule the garden, are fluorescent even in the fog. The dill sways, bejewelled with dew. Zucchinis are not far off and soon there will be bushels. Slugs suck at potato plant leaves but can't do much damage now that things are this far along. Soon the sun will make them burrow – if the sun ever comes back.

I assume it's the Bermuda High, an offshore high pressure system that brings good weather to Nova Scotia, somewhere that is keeping the ocean cool and providing good conditions for coastal fog. But my garden likes the fog, as do I. We are damp and celebratory, both of us. The marsh is singing – sparrows and finches. The smallest birds around here are the ones who sing the sweetest. One lone bittern is poking his head skyward, pretending he is a plant but when he spies a minnow in the shallow stream, he darts for it and misses.

For death is on holiday here near the end of July. And the wild tiger lilies, fully aware of this, are about to burst into a private symphony of orange.

July 30

Forgotten Among the Lilies

I woke up at six this morning and took the dog to the beach to see a grey flying carpet of mist bisecting the rising sun. I wanted to get my surfboard and wetsuit and go surfing but I had a radio interview lined up for 7:30 so I just savoured with all my five senses the broad, empty low-tide beach, the salted light, the sea with its small perfect waves. There was not a breath of wind but the air was generous to my morning lungs.

My interview was by phone with local CBC host Don Connolly. The provincial election was only a week away and I was trying to add another issue to the agenda: school libraries. So far, the campaigns focussed on tax cuts, car insurance, hospitals and even classrooms. But not school libraries. Only 61 percent of Nova Scotia high school students had ever taken a book out of their school library, a recent survey concluded. Nearly all full-time teacher-librarians had been cut or relegated to classrooms. Volunteers ran most school libraries and there was almost no money for new books. And kids had little interest in the old dusty ones from the sixties, fifties and before.

Having made my case before the radio public, I was now free to surf. The water was a mere seven degrees as the result of a cruel summer upwelling that was keeping all the North Atlantic colder than usual. A young man I had known when he was a kid paddled out; Jake, now studying finance at the University of Hawaii, was back home for a visit. He was headed towards a life as a professional volleyball player. Volleyball had landed him a scholarship. It would be his career, he said, until his knees gave out. Then he'd use his knowledge of money to pick up the slack. The water was a shock to his system. A surfer from Quebec paddled out to join us. I paddled hard and slid down the smooth face of a glassy, cold Nova Scotia wave. I set up for the tiny tube of the shore break, tucked low to let the hungry little wave swallow me for breakfast and spit me out onto the sand of the beach here at the reef.

Another phone interview with a *Chronicle-Herald* writer followed as soon as I got out of the shower at home. And before the day was over I had all three political parties preparing to make public commentary on where they stood on this ignored issue. By now I was referring to librarians as the "guardian angels of books" and school libraries were the "sanctuaries of knowledge" in a school. I had been to dozens of schools around the province. Those libraries, I had discovered, had been "gutted," a verb that the *Herald* reporter borrowed for his headline. Good man.

When that interview concluded I was again free to spend my morning alone in my garden, with books and birds and the great twelve-billion-year-old random universe. But I opted to make one more call – a cold call this time to another daily newspaper, so I had to put on full verbal regalia to make my pitch. I put forward a practised, paced and a polished pitch: stats, studies, the state of school libraries and finally something personal. "When I was maybe thirteen," I told the young woman reporter, "I thought I was losing my mind. I thought I was crazy. I was worried, real worried. Somehow, my school librarian saw this in my face and steered me to the right books. *The Catcher in the Rye, Catch 22*, and even the darkest of the writings of Mark Twain. Then it became clear that it wasn't me who was crazy, it was the whole freaking world. I think

I was okay after that. I think she might have saved my life."

All the while, the garden waited.

Our well was just about out of water. It is a fairly shallow well, maybe twelve feet deep, as far as the bedrock will allow. Snakes find their way down inside in the summer and you have to put a ladder in, climb down and catch them one by one. I don't really mind them there, although some family members claim our water tastes like snakes. Unfortunately, I sometimes discover dead ones in the bottom and if I don't fish them out soon enough, they decompose and some think this makes for poor drinking water.

The well water problem – lack of water, not snakes – meant that we hadn't done any laundry in a long while. We had a true mountain of it and my daughter Sunyata had volunteered to haul it all to a laundromat. We were loading the dirty laundry into her car when the Jehovah's Witnesses arrived. They had been coming to my house once or twice a year for the past 28 years. We had bought the old farmhouse from one of their own, Rhoda Roast. Rhoda had been generous to us, I believe. We paid what she was asking, $14,900 and she offered to sell us some of the antique furniture in the house. We didn't really have any money left but made puny offers for dressers and chairs and even an old commode. She accepted and a lot of the old stuff stayed put in the house. (The barn, however, she needed for a horse, and a couple of old boys with a tractor somehow hoisted it and towed it away.)

Something about the fact that Rhoda had lived here meant that the Jehovah's Witnesses were committed right on into this next century to convert my children and me. It was a lost cause but they didn't seem to care. They wanted to give us a fair shot at getting into their heaven whether we wanted it or not.

So they were still showing up on a grand sunny summer day like this in 2003. I was shirtless and barefoot and the man had a suit on while the woman looked like she'd just attended church on a crisp cloudless day in 1953. They were handing out the latest

Watchtower magazines. One was about poverty and focussed on weather. The fact that there was so much poverty and so many weather calamities, they said, was because we were in our final days and that was okay because when the world ended, the good folks would go to the "next kingdom." As the woman pointed out, "What else is there to look forward to?"

Me, I was just trying to make it across the road into my garden so I could study birds and insects. But I was the consummate gentleman and promised I would read all about the crisis in poverty and weather, although the literature would not convince me that the poverty was worse and the weather more cataclysmic than ever before in history. I did believe, however, that both needed fixing as did the problem with school libraries, but I wasn't about to enter into a dialogue on this. I knew the Witnesses believed only Jehovah could fix this stuff and I thought we should, even though I knew we were doing a crummy job. I believed that I had already learned from experience that if you had a couple of snakes in your well, you couldn't just hang back and wait for God to remove the snakes. You had to just grit your teeth, put the aluminium ladder down the well and go catch the suckers and take them someplace else. Even if it scared you.

Believe it or not, all this happened before ten o'clock and then suddenly, the Witnesses were gone, the laundry was off to town and I rewarded myself with a cup of dark roast coffee. Carrying it and a handful of books, a notebook, a pen and the old navy blanket my mother had saved from the Second World War, I walked down my driveway and across the road, past the hundred-year-old Acadian shed that photographers love, to settle on the grass in the sun beside my garden.

I drank my coffee by the cornflowers and the tall, thin, elegant dill plants, still beaded up with morning dew. Although the grass is mowed around the garden, this sacred plot is nestled in the salt marsh at the base of Lawrencetown Lake, surrounded by chest-high vegetation. To a casual observer it may seem as if the garden has been carved out of the great tall ambitious grasses of the marsh. It is one version of Eden (but without snakes, since they all prefer my well) and I always love being alone here with my eyes and ears and nose working overtime.

If pestilence and hurricanes would consume the world tomorrow, then this was my time to savour what nature was providing here and now. The message seemed pretty loud and clear: everything was perfect.

I lay down and studied the planet from ground level. It was a different place from the one I was familiar with – for quite a few years now I had been studying the place from six feet above the surface. Down this low everything was different. It was a green and busy universe. An ant took this opportunity to travel across my notebook page. It was not a straight journey but a mad meandering. I crawled closer to the garden and tucked my head under some grand zucchini leaves, wide as dinner plates and like something from a tropical rainforest. There were fluttering poplar trees from a thin, hopeful sapling I'd transplanted down here two years ago. The jewelweed was in full bloom and so were the tiger lilies. The evidence was obvious: winter had never existed, could never exist. I'd hear no arguments to persuade me otherwise.

Still lying at ground level, looking up at the wispy clouds, I wondered why I did not do this more often. I shunted a pang of Protestant work-ethic guilt off into the thick weeds. This was, after all, my true vocation. I was working. My open books assured me that this was research. A lone sparrow, the only bird in evidence, dangled from a branch and sang a trilling note so sweet, I thought I would melt into the soil and live the rest of my days with grubs and earthworms. And then he was gone.

I cracked open a book I'd bought from a book sale at the library in Sydney, Cape Breton. It was titled *A Field Book on Insects* by Frank E. Lutz, published in 1918. The book was dedicated "To my entomological colleagues" and has a quote at the beginning by the Reverend J.G. Wood who stated, "The study of entomology… lays open to us another world, of which we have been hitherto unconscious, and shows us that the tiniest insect, so small perhaps that the unaided eye can scarcely see it, has work to do in the world, and does it."

The final three words haunted me. It implies there is no dilly-dallying among insects. No whining and complaining. Work is all that matters and they bloody well get on with it, rain or shine. It took a few minutes of mental gymnastics for me to convince myself again that I was truly doing my job by being here. This was all part of my great patchwork of ideas and experiences that would make sense and awaken me (if not others) to knowledge, possibly even knowledge "heretofore" unexpressed.

I had always intended to some day draw my attention to the bug world and here was my opportunity. I could only whole-heartedly agree with Frank Lutz who wrote in his introduction, "All of us are immensely indebted to those who have gone before us. The mass of knowledge about insects, great in reality but small in comparison with our ignorance, has been accumulated, bit by bit, by the labouring man in his Sunday strolls and by the highly-trained investigator." I felt stirred by such words and felt that I too was joining that parade of strollers and investigators out to rid the world of ignorance when it came to our understanding of black flies and dung beetles.

I kept hoping a horned beetle would walk across my navy blanket but no such luck. Even mosquitoes seemed absent on this magnificent morning. Clearly, the point was not to get too focussed on any one thing. A few quarrelling birds demanded my attention but they quickly sailed up into the heavens as soon as my gaze fell upon them. They were in no mood to have me eavesdropping on their altercations.

Perhaps Leonardo da Vinci's advice was to be heeded: "Hence as you go through the fields, turn your attention to various objects, and in turn look now at this thing and now at that, collecting a store of divers facts selected and chosen from those of less value..." Certainly I would continue to collect my "store of divers facts" come what may.

Still committed to my random approach to studying myself and the world around me, I turned to *The Canadian World Almanac* that I had brought along to the garden. My plan was to have a set of books that was as "divers" as my library would allow. Hence, Lutz, Peterson with his birds, da Vinci, plus a book on death and dying and the *Almanac*. If I was going to aspire to da Vinci's Renaissance man status, I needed breadth and hoped depth would follow.

A random "dive" into the *Almanac* revealed that in 1908 and 1909 there were seven Canadian executions each year for crimes committed. As if quotas were being readjusted, there were thirteen each year in 1909 and 1910 before dropping back to seven in 1911. Executioners were quite busy by 1919, celebrating that year with a full nineteen executions. All executions were by hanging, just like in eighteenth-century Halifax when the rope was the preferred way to punish true scoundrels and pirates, although in those days the event was public and viewed as high entertainment.

Through the 1920s and 1930s, sixes and sevens seemed to be the popular number of hangings in Canada until the 1940s when the numbers bumped up to ten and then fourteen. After that the executioner's rope was tested less and less until Canada's final execution, a double hanging of Ronald Turpin and Arthur Lucas in 1962, the year the TransCanada Highway officially opened.

A garden on a bright summer day may seem like a poor place to contemplate capital punishment but I know that a truly skilled theoretical mathematician could do something with those execution statistics and correlate them to the same rise and fall of the population of dill plants in my garden. Some years there are many (all repopulating themselves automatically) and some years there are few. The same holds true for the population of sea urchins and starfish in the sea nearby. The numbers of everything seem to ebb and flow. And one could study these patterns. Sometimes there are logical explanations. Sometimes those explanations cannot be found.

None here today were awaiting the return of the death penalty. But pondering concerns about mortality, I was prompted to get up and stretch my legs for a walk around the perimeter of the garden.

As you probably remember, I have deer in the neighbour-hood who occasionally devour what I have planted: pea plants decimated, Swiss chard chewed to the roots, beets lifted from the soil, chewed and consumed. The deer even carelessly trample the calendula.

Never once have I considered capital punishment for such offences. The deer are lovely and noble beasts and I observe them on misty mornings running through the marsh or just standing there on the gravel road like statues. I generally admire the deer and curse them only when they invade my garden. And I don't want to construct a fence to keep them out. How ugly. Someone once told me that if I put a stake on each corner of the garden and ran a string around it at ankle length, the deer would never go into my garden. This story came from an elderly friend who rarely told me the truth. He pretended to be an expert on everything and usually his knowledge proved to be wrong or flimsy. He claimed to have lived in the far north and had bizarre stories about how he fended off wildlife. "I sprinkled egg shells around anywhere I wanted to keep the porcupines away from. It worked every time.

"Mountain lion urine sprinkled around the back door would keep the bears away. It worked like a charm." He never told me where he got the mountain lion piss. It was just a given that it was easy to come by.

This ancient friend of mine was the one who told me about the string. "Deer hate to have anything touching their ankles. They'll never go in your garden."

Well, I wanted to believe him so I tried it and, strangely enough, it worked quite well. Deer did seem to have pretty delicate ankles and they would wander all around my garden but not want to take a chance on the string. Heck, it wasn't even string; it was some kind of polyester yarn bought at a yard sale. So, with the deer fearing the string on their ankles, the Swiss chard this summer had already grown to historic proportions. The beets were the size of softballs, the peas prolific and the dill tall and feathery as the clouds in the sky. The string around the garden was working and it would continue to work as long as I believed in it. If I stopped believing in sensitive deer ankles, it would be all over in one night. The yarn and me had a force field going and that's all there was to it.

A quick survey of the morning garden revealed the first zucchini of the year, a ten-inch missile of a thing, the first of many large phallic fruits to follow. My Egyptian onions were as tall as me and sporting those tiny miniature onion tops with great curlicue green sprouts. The calendula flowers were trying to take over: strength in numbers, more orange than yellow, happy campers all of them. Certain weeds I had allowed to remain: dandelion, chickweed, pigweed and samphire. But this year's samphire was diminished to a mere three plants. I had thinned this delicate, spindled, edible plant too harshly the year before. It had been like the year 1919 for samphire.

I had left one wild plantain growing from a pile of rotting seaweed in the middle of the garden. Also known by the native people as "Englishman's foot" it had been one of the few plants to grow where the leathered white man's shoes had trampled. My lone plantain was like a great green lotus flower there in the middle of my garden and I wondered if it would produce enough seeds to overrun the place next time around.

I sat down in the middle of the garden by the great plantain plant and read from *The Tibetan Book on Living and Dying* by

Sogyal Rinpoche. He agreed with Elisabeth Kubler-Ross that there were five clear stages to dying: denial, anger, bargaining, depression and acceptance.

There was only one surprise to me on that list: bargaining. I wondered if that was universal. It seemed like a very American concept – trying to buy your way out of a situation. Sure, I could see someone who was deeply religious trying to bargain with God. "I will be good from here on, if you just let me live." But if you didn't believe in God, with whom did you bargain?

I would give this more thought. Sogyal Rinpoche also pointed out that some people needed "permission" to die and a chill went through me, thinking of recent people I had known who died and how true this seemed to be. It was certainly appropriate but also gracious and childlike. Picking your time of death when the others around you are ready to let you go.

In a Mi'kmaq spiritual ceremony, smoke is offered to the four corners of the world – north, south, east, west. Smoke ascending to the heavens symbolizes a connection between earth and heaven. A pipe may be smoked in a ceremony and the person who carries the pipe is an elder of responsibility. He or she does not own the pipe; he just carries it and passes it on to the next generation. The sacredness of tobacco led to leniency on the part of the Canadian government when it came to taxes on tobacco. Based on very old treaties, Aboriginals are exempt from paying sales taxes on cigarettes so they can buy them much more cheaply than other nicotine addicts. The obvious health problems result.

When tobacco was first becoming popular in England in the very early 1600s, an anonymous poet compared tobacco to love. "Love makes men sail from shore to shore / so doth tobacco," he notes at one point and later on, "Love makes men scorn all coward fears/ so doth tobacco." Only this past month did Halifax make a hard-line stand on the weed, creating a stringent no smoking law applied to restaurants and even bars where more than a few smokers remain in open defiance of the crackdown. Such official criticism of tobacco was preceded several centuries before by no less than King James I who said that smoking was "A custom loathsome to the eye, harmful to the brain, dangerous to the lungs, and in the black stinking fume thereof, resembling the Stygian smoke pit that is bottomless." Nuff said.

Standing by my garden I read on page 263 of my 1991 *World Almanac* a "roster" of nations belonging to the UN. Out of 159 members, twenty countries begin with the letter "S", sixteen with the letter "B", sixteen with "C", and thirteen with the letter "M". When it comes to nationhood and politics, "S", "B", "C" and "M" are far and away the most popular sounds to attach to the name of your home and native land.

I returned to the navy blanket, determined to continue my thwarted responsibility to the study of insects. I was feeling another pang of guilt as if my diversions were disappointing the legions of amateur entomologists who had gone before me. Only da Vinci would approve of my randomness, even perhaps approve of my string theory, and my study of execution numerology and nation names. As I waited, though, no bugs presented themselves to inspire me, so I retreated to the Renaissance, opening my *Renaissance Reader* bought in 1969 as a used book for a mere 40 cents (original retail price a full $1.65). There are 756 pages in the book. Even at retail, the cost was .2 cents per page. At the used book price, it was .05 cents per page or one ten-thousandth of a dollar per page.

Whoever owned the book before me, probably a university student, had pencilled in on the contents page the title of a Carole King song, "Will You Still Love Me Tomorrow?" And this made me wonder if it was just the name of the song or had someone, mid-class, written this note to a lover and then waited for a response. Certainly this question was as relevant to the twentieth-century lovers as it had been to those of the Renaissance.

As the morning moved I felt a quiet but tangible thrill from having carved out this pocket of time for contemplation, for reading, for exploring the world in the most random way. There were blossoming cumulous clouds to the north now, white fluffy ships, sailing on higher winds, sure to be storm clouds by the afternoon but presently still nothing more than voluminous blossoms in the northern sky.

My journey from six in the morning to twelve noon had never taken me more than a kilometre from my bed. A random thumbing through the *Renaissance Reader* left me with these final words from St. John of the Cross in his poem "Obscure Night of the Soul" wherein he says,

> All ceased and I was not,
> Leaving my cares and shame
> Among the lilies, and forgetting them.

The *cares*, that is, and the *shame*. Forgotten among the lilies, the tiger lilies in this case, and the calendula, the jewelweed and the lowly plantain.

August 1

Big Tancook Island

B ig Tancook Island is about seven miles to sea from the town of Chester, Nova Scotia. It takes about 45 minutes to get there on a ferry that charges five dollars for the round trip. I'd been out to Tancook four times before and each time it was like being delivered into another country. Not exactly like going back in time but more like turning up in an alternate reality – a what-if kind of place that prompted me to use it as the basis for the fictional island I called Ragged Island in a novel called *Sea of Tranquility*.

I live a single life in two geographies: one real, one fabricated for fiction. Tancook, as it exists, is so close to fictional possibilities that it didn't take much to leap one step further. Because I hadn't been back to Tancook since the novel came out, I was more familiar with my recreated Ragged Island than its predecessor so I hoped to now compare them and make notes. It was a warm, clear day as my friend Lou Costanzo and I stood on the deck of the *William G. Ernst*, and I watched a cormorant dive down beneath the boat in the clear green water at the Chester dock.

Chester is posh for Nova Scotia. A lot of summer money flows through the town, so much so that Lou was lured into a coffee bar touting cappuccino from freshly ground beans. Buddy behind the counter was too busy talking to some Americans about selling his sailboat so Lou never did get his cappuccino. The ferry was said to leave promptly on schedule.

When we ambled on board, big metal crates were being loaded with a crane operated by a young man in a hard hat. They allowed one truck on board with some digging equipment in the back. Later we would find the truck and its workmen digging a grave with the machine, some sort of gas powered Honda thing, state of the art. A full day's job – ferry to the island, dig a grave and shuttle home for dinner.

Sailing from Chester, we passed one all-too-stately mansion owned by a man who'd made his fortune in fish and then we passed an island with another half-hidden mansion owned by Christopher Ondaatje, whose massive fortune, I presumed, was based on investing inheritance money and reaping rewards.

Although Lou was probably tired of hearing my literary woes, I told him that a review had appeared recently in the *Globe and Mail* chastising *Sea of Tranquility* for not being cynical enough, suggesting a book that made you feel good was not at all suited to the twenty-first century. Another of my book projects (a non-fiction one intending to be humorous) had recently been rejected by a big New York publisher quite politely with the note from the editor saying that he had hoped it to be "more side-splitting." Apparently, I was trying to hold down some middle ground of being optimistic and entertaining when I should have been trying to be dark, hard-bitten and hilarious enough to make you drop to your knees.

Looking out at the serene blue waters of Mahone Bay, Lou, the psychologist by profession, shrugged and suggested I piss on them all, which was his well-planned way of reminding me it was his day off and I would not get any free therapy for my minor woes.

With that settled, a growing zephyr snatched a cap emblazoned with a bulldozer from the head of a fellow pilgrim and placed it properly upon the wake of the ferry as we were passing a point of land with three straggly black spruce trees. The cap would not be retrieved and I am sure the wind was known to be a dependable thief in these parts, a good sea breeze wanting a mainlander's cap as often as it can get away with it. I was hatless as usual and immune to all but the slight chill of the wind, which Lou assured me was not even strong enough for windsurfing.

I think Lou had wanted to bring bikes and ride around the island because he kept telling me we should see "the whole thing at once, as a piece." I was more in favour of a slower pace and had my eye set on the arm of land beyond the South East Cove. I had a rustic map that had inspired me to head towards a place called "The Kaffel" and beyond that "The Ovens." I was, of course, also looking for Sylvie, the eighty-year-old woman of my novel who had out-lived four husbands. I had planned on her outliving five husbands but after the fourth one died on her, I had decided enough was enough. It was Sylvie, after all, not me, who had been way too optimistic for the Toronto critic, and any spirit of her I could find on Tancook would suit me just fine.

On the Internet, the night before, I had come across this official posting from the Nova Scotia Department of Transportation for November of 1997. (As you've probably discovered, all manner of out-of-date information is left floating around on the Internet.) It read:

> Workers discovered corrosion on the centre of the permanent ferry, *William G. Ernst*, as it was undergoing a regular scheduled refit earlier this month. For safety, the crane was removed and new parts ordered. The parts, which had to be ordered from Austria, will take 13 weeks to be delivered.

> Residents of Tancook can transport cargo on the *Scotian* ferry, which will act as replacement. A school bus placed on the *Scotian* offers an enclosed place for riders to sit during their crossing.

> Bill Yarn, Transportation and Public Works.

I'd actually seen the *Scotian* without the school bus on board back at the Chester dock. It was a medium-sized flat barge of sorts and I can imagine what a solemn affair the crossing would have been in the winter of 1997, sitting in a school bus parked in the centre of that barge, pushing through heaving seas under a grey leaden sky.

I liked the fact that Mr. Yarn had chosen the verb "discovered" instead of the less muscular "found." It prompted a vision of sweaty men doing hard, serious work in their inspection and one of them, lifting his own bulldozer cap and saying, "Bill, you better get down here and see this."

Bill Yarn knew corrosion when he saw corrosion and what would you expect from a crane anchored on steel decking with salt water sloshing on it day after day. Why the part had to come from Austria is a bit of a mystery. Government employees are often accused of tendering contracts to friends and relatives. So it was either an attempt to prove once and for all that there was no such thing going on here or the opposite. Germans had settled Tancook and much of this shore. A cousin perhaps in the Tyrol had a crane repair business. The part would take thirteen weeks to get here while Tancookers sat on an idling school bus (to keep the chill off) for the crossings.

The word Tancook either means "the big island" or "facing the open sea," both derived from the Mi'kmaq people who had the run of this place until the English started mucking things up in the mid eighteenth century. In 1759, the island was granted to Patrick Sutherland, Esq., who failed to perform some obligation required to keep the island, so he lost it. George Grant and John Henry Flieger were given the whole shebang after that. Their professions were described, respectively, as "merchant" and "gentleman." In this century we often wonder what exactly a gentleman did to earn his keep. My guess is that he did squat but someone owed him a favour.

A surveyor did everyone the favour of checking the island over in 1788, just twelve years after the American Revolution, and said, "Great Tancook contains 550 acres of land. It is a general good hardwood land, beech, birch, maple and some oak and ash... upon moderate calculation there may be about ten thousand cords of wood and some timber."

Nova Scotia had in those days, one hell of a lot of trees – hardwood and softwood. Tancook seemed like a fairly remote place to be hauling stove wood from but the English were here to consume whatever could be consumed and pretty soon someone would start harvesting those beech trees. I heat my own house with firewood and, on average, I use two cords of hardwood a year, although on a really cold and super windy night, the wood burns so quickly that it seems like I might as well just throw the logs up the chimney and be done with it.

If I were to have had access to all that firewood, I reckon that the trees of Tancook would have heated my house for five thousand years and still left a few trees standing. It was a considerable resource. Should all that cordage have been delivered at once, it would have made a fair mountain of fuel and I would have been the envy of all the woodstove owners on the Eastern Shore where good beech and ash wood is relatively rare.

The man who asked for the ferry fare was bearded and sunburnt with a happy paunch drooped over his belt. A kind of summer South Shore Santa Claus who chatted and laughed and didn't seem to have a care in the world. When we arrived at Little Tancook Island, the first stop, he reached out with a long metal pole for a rope that he tied onto a bulkhead on the ship much as they did in the *Titanic* movie but on a much less grand scale.

Little Tancook was, as the name implied, smaller than Big Tancook and I had walked the entire perimeter of it once in a couple of hours, dawdling at that. Five people got on and six got off. Within five minutes we were free of the place and headed to our destination across a big channel separating Big from Little. I wondered if there was any animosity or competition between the people of Big and Little Tancook Islands and hoped there was no prejudice of any sort but my experience with human nature suggested otherwise.

There was quite the hubbub ashore at Big Tancook with cars all jammed up on the wharf tight enough so that it was hard to actually weave through them once off the boat. The once-corroded crane was put to good use as Lou and I set out on foot for the Kaffel.

Traffic from the wharf roared by, drivers having picked up family or relatives now speeding on down the dusty gravel roads. Each vehicle uniformly lacked two of the usual accoutrements of mainland cars: no licences and no mufflers. Some seemed to be driven by boys as young as fourteen. I was satisfied that in some regards civilization had not caught up with Tancookers. Back on the mainland, an election campaign was being waged between the three parties and the main issue was the high cost of car insurance. I was fairly certain not a blessed soul on this island was losing any sleep over that one.

Nonetheless, houses sported political placards in the front yards. The Conservatives must have ruled on Tancook. John Chataway was the favoured candidate here. I never fully understood the posting of those lawn placards. Was it an attempt to advertise your favourite candidate or just proclaim your politics? As Lou and I hiked further and further from the harbour, the signs seemed even harder to figure when it came to purpose.

We walked past the cemetery where we saw the truck from the boat and the men using the Honda machine to dig a grave. This was the very Baptist cemetery that I had fixed in my mind and used in my novel. Here is where Sylvie had buried her four husbands, returned to clean lichen off gravestones with bleach and a toothbrush. Here is where she had experienced grief, acceptance and even hope.

Sylvie Young had once been married to David Young, and lo and behold, here in the real world of Tancook, was a headstone for David Young. I don't know if I had seen that headstone before and used the real name or if it was a fluke but it sent a small thrill down my spine.

A fiction writer, on occasion, is not sure which world he prefers to live in, the real one or the one he has created in his head. Here on Tancook, today, the lines were blurring and that was fine by me. Maybe I could live in both. The burdock on Tancook was as tall as the burdock on Ragged Island and the burrs would stick to your pants equally well in either place.

I'm sorry to say that there were more fields of cabbage growing on Ragged Island than on contemporary Tancook. This place had once been the land where cabbage was king.

The first families to actually settle here were mostly German farmers. They liked an island because they could let their cows, goats, pigs, sheep and oxen run freely. Rarely did ox stumble off the short cliffs and fall into the sea. Oxen were slow but they were not thought of as stupid. People got drunk on occasion, however, fell from the rocks into the water and drowned but not farm animals. This was a known fact.

The German farmers down through the years became renowned for the cabbages they grew – some the size of bushel baskets, others merely the size of basketballs – and also the sauerkraut they made. Sauerkraut is a highly salted, belly-bloating dish that is addicting to the island and mainland folks of Lunenburg County. It's part of this county's historical record and in Judge DesBrisay's highly touted *History of the County of Lunenburg*, he writes, "In November, 1894, Mr. Sylvester Baker of Tancook Island pulled two cabbages from his field, one of which weighed 25 ½ pounds and another 23 ½ pounds." Like me, the Tancook farmers hauled seaweed to rot in their gardens and replenish the soil and it did good work as a fertilizer.

More than a hundred years ago, mainland schooners pulled up to the docks and Tancookers sold these monster cabbages, and the islanders also made many, many barrels of sauerkraut to send off to Europe.

Although the brand name of Tancook Sauerkraut lives on emblazoned on the quart-sized milk cartons it is sold in, there are only a few backyard gardens left that we observed with cabbages the size of mere soccer balls. The old cabbage fields are ruled by bull thistle, burdock, pigweed and timothy and the swayback barns have a forgotten and forlorn look to them. My guess is that the world has moved on to other pleasures beyond feasting on sauerkraut. I've heard old-timers speak of sitting down to a plateful of sauerkraut and they spoke with such enthusiasm about the event as if they had experienced some kind of elevated amphetamine high. It couldn't have just been the salt. My guess is that the love of sauerkraut and the experience of the sauerkraut rush will not be remembered far into this century. And that too will be a loss. There are no sauerkraut franchises popping up on the mainland and shelf space for sauerkraut has diminished in the superstores in recent years.

Our road had diminished to a dirt trail as we neared the farthest point of land, the "end" of Tancook Island known as the Kaffel, which we would later learn means "the rocks by the sea." The final house had an NDP sign on its lawn. The NDP candidate had a serious German-sounding name: Heinrich Bitter-Suerman. He would end up coming in a close second in the provincial race. His name made me think of an unhappy man at a difficult occupation but it turned out that he was a transplant surgeon and a good one at that. I don't know which organ he specialized in transplanting, but he had one strong supporter at the near end of human civilization here at the cusp of the Atlantic. The *Daily News* profile would indicate his marital status as "single," and for children, it indicated he had six.

They say there are 365 islands in Mahone Bay, one for each day of the year but I have not counted them myself so you'll have to take this as hearsay. Tancook is the largest and, given its "favourable aspects," it was once a great sailing port. The Tancook whalers were schooners built here in that previous, more favourable century. The sails were soaked in a dye made from spruce bark, which made them brown instead of white but preserved them from rot. Some Tancookers were great sailing men. In Alison Mitcham's *Offshore Islands of Nova Scotia and New Brunswick*, she includes an "old-timer's" account of sailing his Tancook schooner:

> In tacking, one man caught the club under his arm and walked around mainmast and hooked sheet on the other side. Woe betides you if you lost your hold on the club! If there was a good breeze you are liable to get your ribs or head cracked.

Woe betides indeed.

According to the same old-timer, if you rejiggered your "staysail" into a "squaresail" (a smart thing to do under certain conditions), it was called "scandalizing the staysail," which I find very charming. Famous island sailors of yore had names like Hip Baker, Al Langille, Leander Young and Zip Wilson.

Once we arrived at the Kaffel we ate a hasty sandwich on the rocks facing straight out to sea, south-southwest by my reckoning. If you had a Tancook schooner with spruce-browned sails and headed out to sea in the direction I was looking, your first landfall would be Antarctica on a voyage that would take you smartly mid-Atlantic between Brazil and Senegal. It was a big blue ocean with only two other islands even visible, the famous Ironbound slightly to the east and Flat Island to the west. Ironbound had once been immortalized (or at least fictionalized) as *Rockbound* in a novel by

Frank Parker Day published in 1928. Day wrote of the place, "In rough weather, when seas broke on the southern bar, spray and blown spume flew clear across the valley to the northern shore." Not exactly paradise. My own Ragged Island was a more picturesque place but then I was prone to putting an optimistic spin on my islands, much to the chagrin of urban critics.

There was no "spray or blown spume" here today. Just sun and sea, but on the worrisome side, we discovered here on the rocky ledge a pair of women's running shoes and two white socks. Whoever had come here wearing them had not put them on again. Lou agreed with me that it looked ominous but that we shouldn't leap to conclusions. It would have been a solitary spot for a suicide swim but it seemed unlikely. The extreme cold of these waters, they say, would make such an impact on you if you immersed yourself without a wetsuit that it would give the most hard-bitten suicides second thoughts. Still we surveyed the clear deep water for evidence of despair and, finding none, decided it was someone who had not walked but driven here past the final political yard posting and simply returned home without footwear.

Because it was there on our map, we both were anxious to walk through the forest to the western shore to find the dot labelled, "The Ovens." We'd seen other "ovens" near Lunenburg and they were magnificent booming caves. However, the only forest trail we found kept dwindling until it came to a small clearing with an extraordinary amount of porcupine shit in the middle. Greatly disappointed, we backtracked and quickly came to the same conclusion; we'd have to bloody hurry if we were to catch our ferry back to the mainland.

It was a forced march past the queued up PC, NDP and Liberal election signs. Early on, Lou shouted to a woman hanging out an exceptional array of laundry (with an elaborate pulley system) if she knew where the Ovens were.

"I know they are there," she said, pointing in the direction of the hill behind her house, "but they're hard to get to. I've lived here my whole life and have never seen them."

Well, we didn't feel so bad. The Ovens would have to wait for us.

We were losing ground and unlikely to make the ferry on time. I thought we might flag down one of the island vehicles for a ride but we fell in with a galloping woman who assured us if we could keep up to her pace, we'd make it. She was from Montreal and said she lived on the island alone, commuting ashore to the ferry and then to a job, a long way off in the Annapolis Valley. She had always wanted to live on an island and here she was. "They don't quite trust you, though, if you are a single woman on an island like this," she said, implying that the local women must have thought she'd come down from Montreal to snatch their fishermen husbands. Perhaps the men thought she smuggled drugs. She wasn't sure how much more she'd last on the island but it wasn't like islanders were unkind to her. Just wary. I never exactly asked her what she did but she struck me as a hospital administrator, one who needed an island to return to after a hard day's work.

Muffler-less cars were all jammed up on the wharf, making it difficult again to actually get onboard but we made it with moments to spare. The trip back was free. You paid your five dollars to Santa Claus on the way over and no one cared if you returned or not. Or if you could find alternate transportation to Big Tancook, you could forever return to the mainland for free. Onboard, the woman from Montreal noted that we'd been ripped off. She buys books of tickets in advance and for anyone who does that the round trip fare is a dollar.

I had the good fortune to sit by a man named Brian Jones who wanted to talk about antlers on the return voyage. He was a pale man with a fresh sunburn and a copy of the *National Post*. We were making small talk about the island and I had told him I'd seen a photograph of a farmer on Tancook who had found a baby moose that had miraculously swam there from the mainland. He had tamed the moose and, in the photo, it was hitched to a winter sled. Another photo had shown the moose hitched to a plough, presumably to plough a field for cabbage to make sauerkraut. These were historical details that had found their way into my novel about Ragged Island. When a really intriguing historical fact sounds like fiction, a novelist can usually just get away with plugging it into his book and readers think he was very clever for making up such a thing.

Mention of the moose got us talking about people crashing into moose with their cars in Newfoundland where Brian had recently been on undisclosed government work. He assured me that if you hit a moose with your car, because of the long legs, the moose "almost always" goes up over the hood of your car and smashes through your windshield. If you are lucky, you are still alive with a dead moose in your lap. Other times, the driver gets killed.

"The best thing you can do up there is tailgate a tractor trailer to avoid hitting a moose. But even that doesn't always work." Brian assured me that moose at night have been known to jump directly between tractor-trailers and speeding cars. "They're that stupid," he said.

Once too often this summer I had pondered how the Americans had allowed the conspiracy that elected George W. Bush (recently publicly called a "shrub" by the premier of Saskatchewan) president and then led them into an unnecessary war. I wanted to explain how a moose darting between a truck and a car at night was nowhere near as stupid as this but I thought it best to keep politics out of it. It had been a lovely day and I didn't want to spoil it.

One thing led to another, though, and pretty soon Brian was admitting that he knew a fair bit about antlers. He'd been up in the Yukon and had personally tripped over a massive pair of elk antlers in the wilderness. Later he had read that male elk shed their massive headgear every year or two. I said that I was pretty sure they went through a personality transition when that happened – identity crisis even. Brian thought I was right on that count.

There was little fanfare when we arrived in Chester. I found the town much as I expected it to be at this time of day. Wealthy people (or at least people who were trying to look like they were wealthy) were sitting deckside at outdoor restaurants, drinking alcoholic beverages or fussing with escarole salads or doing nothing at all. We were already a long way from Tancook Island.

On our walk back to the car, I told Lou that I wished it was the year 1821 and it was winter.

Lou was hoping to find that coffee bar and see if the proprietor had concluded his sailboat conversation and was prepared to make a good cup of cappuccino but I was lobbying for the Tim Hortons up at Chester Basin. He sighed and asked me the obvious. "Why winter? Why 1821?"

"Because that was the year Mahone Bay froze rock solid from Chester to Big Tancook."

"Impossible," he said.

"But true." It was an extraordinary event. Frederick Clattenburg took it in his head to walk out to Tancook from the mainland and did just that but after becoming disoriented on the ice he died of what they say was "fatigue." He was found dead on the ice in the channel between Big and Little Tancook.

Chestertonians that winter ice-skated to Tancook and then on to a place called Murder's Point on Winters Island and came back ashore near Lunenburg.

In 1846, she iced up good again and people were hauling "puncheons of molasses and barrels of flour" by horse across Mahone Bay. In March of that year, ice still thick, a man named Lot Church took his horse and sleigh to Tancook and on to Blandford on the mainland, the home of the contemporary junkyard that looks like a lighthouse from sea due to all those glaring windshields. One of Lot's neighbours, Charles Lordly, Esq. was out on the ice hauling hay and other goods with his oxen, sometimes checking the thickness of the ice with a hand auger and discovered he could drill up to two feet deep and not even hit water.

Winters aren't like that any more. You'd be taking a pretty poor gamble if you wanted to take your pet ox out on any of the bays along any of the shores of Nova Scotia even in February. With the heyday of the sauerkraut years behind us and the winters so warm, it begins to make a person feel like the best years are all behind us. My guess is that once you start seeing official Nova Scotia licence plates on the old Chevettes and Ford trucks of Tancook, it will all be over but the shouting.

August 17

Paris, Polypropylene and Yellow Patches

The dark shadow of depression was creeping up on me from the left this week. I saw it stalking but didn't want to turn and confront it directly. Late summer breeds this sort of thing for some reason and I felt the dark tide tugging me into its current. I vowed to keep my distance from the predator.

I'd been preparing for a CBC TV talk show and, the day of the taping before an audience, I felt ready to hold my own ground with the other guests – Lloyd Axeworthy, former Minister of Foreign Affairs and Warren Kinsella, an advisor to Jean Chrétien. We would be discussing the events leading up to the Treaty of Versailles in Paris in 1919, a treaty that set Europe and the rest of the world onto a near inevitable cataclysm of a second world war. Beyond that, conflicts happening today in Palestine and Iraq were the result of decisions made by a handful of gentlemen in that place far and away.

While the TV cameras rolled, I set aside my own woes to talk intelligently about the woes of the past. Thinking about those political gentlemen in great drawing rooms, parcelling up the world, however, sobered me into considering the possibility that certain patterns in history, certain man-made catastrophes, war even, are truly inevitable. This is something I would not like to believe. I had formed a powerful personal mythology, shaped by growing up in the United States, shaped by a bubble of intellectual optimism cultivated mid-century, that suggested *nothing* was inevitable. All things were possible. A single individual with the right commitment and ability *could* change the world. For the better.

Woodrow Wilson failed to muster the support at home for the League of Nations. The U.S. did not join. The League drowned in its own good intentions and failed. President Wilson, his health worn down by the work in Paris, by the lack of support for his peace plan at home, had a stroke and eventually died.

While I was gabbing in a TV studio, back home on the Eastern Shore, tragedy struck at nearby Rocky Run, a narrow channel running beneath the trestles of an old abandoned railway bridge. A young man of twenty-three had launched his kayak in the deep calm pool on the Porter's Lake side of the bridge and followed the swift tidal current out to sea. While his family watched, however, his kayak caught sideways on one of the creosote covered pylons and became jammed. Unable to get out of the kayak, the polypropylene craft began to bend around the post, pinning the young man's legs inside the boat and pulling him underwater.

The people on shore screamed for help and a couple of surfers who had been driving nearby heard the shouts. They plunged into the water and tried to extricate the kayaker, only to be ripped away and pulled downstream by the overwhelmingly powerful force of the water emptying out of Porter's Lake into the sea. The tide was near low and there was a full moon. Two elemental forces beyond anyone's control made the current incessant and powerful.

My friend, who I will call Leander, was working at his garage not far away and heard the screaming. He ran to see what was going on and joined in the effort to help the submerged victim. The kayak was bent further now, wrapped around the pylon. No tugging could release it or the man caught in its grip. Leander tied a rope on one end of the kayak but it slipped free as he and others tried to tug at it.

Leander and the other would-be rescuers stayed on, trying to work against the relentless current, watching the trapped victim a mere foot or two underwater, until the fire company rescuers arrived. But by then it was too late.

I had kayaked myself in Rocky Run but never chanced the paddle underneath the trestles there. At high tide, it would have been a simple manoeuver with only the gentle tug of seawater one way or the other but at low tide, it was a whole different story. Having once been involved in an attempt to save a drowning woman at sea, I have always felt a personal connection to any water tragedy in my neighbourhood, a kind of illogical responsibility. After all, I play in the sea. I surf. I kayak. I taunt various dangers and judge my limits, so far always seeing the perimeter of true danger with clarity. This is either a practised skill or it is an illusion.

The young man's tragedy encouraged my dark stalker to pick up the pace, taunting me perhaps, wanting me back in its grip. I knew this summer, my fifty-second, to be a rite of passage for me from one phase of my life to another but it was unclear which way I was going. It was obvious I could head in any number of directions.

Was part of me jammed up at the pylon, carried there by a relentless inevitable tide? Part of me was hanging back, for sure, in the safe calm, deep waters I was familiar with. My boat stable, my spirits buoyant, but cautious and wise. Part of me was already through the trestles, feeling the rush of water and adrenalin that comes with sliding through death's grasping hands and facing the open sea, wind up the nostrils, salt water spray cool and clean on the face.

My family and I decided to go inland for a couple of days where we stayed at a cottage in the serene, orchard-filled Gaspereau Valley. Our rented cottage was in a broad field. Horses, ponies and chickens walked around the front yard. Hummingbirds alighted on a feeder on the front porch. It was a time of hiatus, repair and recharging.

My daughters and I hiked the rim of dykes built along the river over three hundred years ago by Acadian farmers. The same Acadians who were driven from their land by the ruling English military in the eighteenth century, sent into exile in the U.S., many of them ending up in Louisiana. There was little evidence left of the brutality of history in this bucolic summer valley but it was buried here, inches beneath in the red soil.

Felicific calculus, sometimes known by the user-friendly term as happiness calculus, or also "hedonic calculus," is based on some ideas by the philosopher Jeremy Bentham. It implies that we decide what is the right thing to do by determining which actions will bring "the greatest happiness for the greatest number of people." In Robert M. Martin's handy *Philosopher's Dictionary* you'll find felicific calculus just three items down on the same page from fascism, which was another kind of human calculus, an authoritarian kind and Martin reminds us that "most philosophers known to us today were hostile to fascism," which is a comforting thought.

Martin Heidegger (pronounced "High-digger") was the exception to that rule. Aside from approving of fascism, Heidegger, an existential phenomenologist by trade, believed that our awareness of our own demise and the fear associated with it is the fundamental tool that shapes who we are.

I for one am not an existential phenomenologist and am happy that M. Heidegger was not one of my surfing buddies or a chance roommate at university. I'm sure he was a smart guy but prone to a bit too much navel gazing in a German existential sort of way.

I knew that books were part of my restorative regimen this summer but I also knew that it was even healthier to get out of the house and proceed with my study of the natural world beyond my doorstep. To that end, I located my *Audubon Society Field Guide to North American Mushrooms* and went in search of these adventurous life forms that the Greeks believed were created by lightning.

My favourite mushroom was the chanterelle and there was a tasty crop of them that grew year after year right behind my old C-band satellite dish as if they had been beamed there from space. My chanterelle crop was a disappointment this year and the ones that had grown bigger than a thimble were eaten by slugs (darn them). I was not interested in looking for more edible fungi but instead seeking to identify heretofore unrecognized mushrooms for my own edification and even enlightenment.

This was my summer to learn something from everything and anything, putting my universe back together piece by piece after it had become unglued. Folks in the Middle Ages who sometimes found circular patterns of mushrooms called them "fairy rings" and thought tiny people of the forest created them. Maybe I would find evidence of the same. I was sure that a close encounter with sprites would greatly improve my attitude towards the world.

The wind was out of the northwest bringing the first early chill of autumn, news that summer, short as it had been, was not going to be around much longer. My first mushroom was yellow but I could not nail down a name for it. I was just warming up. There were great colonies of Indian peace pipes like the ones I had seen in my youth and near them prolific communities of something called crested coral, a kind of Calvaria. I had seen them often in the woods but just thought they were "some kind of fungus," having grown elitist over the years as to which life forms deserved my attention and which did not.

Crested coral, if you got down on your hands and knees, actually did look like coral and it was quite beautiful with its many spiky branches and "toothed tips." The book said it was edible but it didn't look desirable so I passed on a taste test. Since I was already at ground level, I crawled along until another mushroom introduced itself to me: a spiny puffball. Puffballs had also been part of my summer childhood and my friends and I abused them by kicking them and watching the cloud produced as if we had detonated a small bomb. There are many more puffballs out there than you and I have ever thought about. To name a few, there are: tumbling puffballs, western lawn puffballs, the fuzzy false truffle, sculptured puffballs, tough puffballs, skull-shaped puffballs, pigskin poison puffballs and gem-studded puffballs. In some university, I am sure, there is a professional mycologist (a scholar who studies fungus) who has dedicated his life to the study of the pigskin poison puffball. There but for the grace of God...

I was wishing that we had giant puffballs in the neighbourhood – the grandfather of all puffballs. They are nearly two feet across and I can only imagine what a good swift kick would unleash. But I'd have to settle for this, a little spiny puffball, a mere two inches across. Even then I could have been wrong about nomenclature, since positive identification "requires seeing all stages of development" and I didn't have that much time on my hands.

I moved on through the mushroom forest until I came across another one of those yellow mushrooms and realized I'd have to sit down and nail him with a name. He was tall and had a large bold yellow cap like a student in the classroom wanting to answer the teacher's question, as if waving his hand frantically, shouting, "Call on me, me, me" and the teacher not wanting to call on him again for the long-winded ludicrous answer he would give.

A bit more study, begrudging this time on my part, revealed that the clown was either yellow patches or yellow-orange fly agaric. The fly one is poisonous but not deadly. If you accidentally gulped one down, however, you'd sweat a lot and feel disoriented, much like my old high school buddy Stanley Campbell during gym class. Yellow patches may or may not be poisonous but the general advice is that it's not worth eating if the mycologists aren't up for making a solid yea or nay. Both are amanitas, lovely word, but certainly a family with a lot of toxic chemicals shared down through the generations.

Somehow it was becoming more interesting now that I knew I was among so many potentially dangerous mushrooms and sure enough, next to rear its deadly smooth shiny self was a pungent fibre head, edibility rated as poisonous. Nothing half-assed about this sucker. It had what they refer to in the mushroom world as a "spermatic odour," and its head was "conical to bell shaped." It was brownish and looked poisonous. Only a fool would set one out at his mushroom buffet. I was now reminded of a luncheon held in my honour with one of the several mayors of Tokyo, an official occasion where I heartily ate all of the prepared fungi set before me. The mayor's official photographer took pictures of me fumbling with my mushrooms and chopsticks. I had trusted them not to serve up amanitas and fibre heads and I guess the trust was warranted. It's funny how you turn over your very life sometimes to people you don't know, whose competence you can't judge, who sometimes you can't even see. I'm thinking of airline pilots. Some of the most wacko guys I ever knew in high school wanted to be pilots and undoubtedly some of them are. It's a scary thought.

Here in the woods, I could at least trust myself *not* to eat the pungent fibre head. Or any of the pungent extended cortinariaceae family, which included Caesar's fibre head, green-foot fibre head, black-nipple fibre head, scaly fibre head, and blushing fibre head. There was also a cinnamon buff cousin known as poison pie and one called corpse finder. A cheerful flamboyant bunch of poison fungi, the lot of them.

Deeper in the forest, away from the intrusion of sunlight and sea breezes I discovered the smaller, thinner, more delicate slimy-veil limacella with their sickly slug-slime brown phallic helmets. According to the Audubon folks, "Formerly known as lepiota glioderma, this species was transferred to the limacella grouping, which accommodates mushrooms with the "slimy universal veil." It was nice of the limacella crowd to be so accommodating.

My interests had been leaning towards the deadly mushrooms, the slimy-veiled and the colourful and I had been bypassing the dull brown loaf-of-bread looking ones that I knew were called boletus. The boletus is mostly edible and apparently sold in gourmet shops around Europe where the citizens are ravenous for the dried version. I myself have lived without a hankering for boletus, all two hundred species of them, but this may change some day. I settled in for a study of the admirable boletus whose edibility is labelled "choice" which prompted me to name this particular mushroom Choyce's boletus but only for notebook purposes. This big puffy boletus had been selected by at least one wild animal as a meal because a big chunk had been eaten from it, prompting me to wonder if an animal has eaten from a mushroom, is that good enough to prove it is edible. I would not put this to any test, however, since I would not be able to observe a wild squirrel or a porcupine after his repast to note its effect. At any rate, the admirable boletus, admirable as it was, looked past its prime and headed towards becoming slug food.

Although the hard-core Ph.D. mycologists all preferred the Latin names and shunned the popular names, the rest of the fungus finding world had had one heck of a good time naming the two hundred varieties of boleta. There was Frost's boletus, named after the poet perhaps, and Zeller's boletus, named for the store. Boleta had descriptive names like spotted, shaggy-stalked, two-coloured, red-cracked, and yellow-cracked but also in the group was chicken-fat. Suillus was another variety, whose taste was only described as "good" and there was one called old man of the woods, then slippery Jack and even a slippery Jill. If you were a taste-testing boletus fanatic (hired perhaps by a Prague gourmet mushroom shop) you could taste a new boletus, one each day, from January right into July before running out of new varieties.

After contemplating a few more mushrooms – inky caps, red-capped saber stalks, tree polypores (all pretending to be the front-half saucer section of the Starship *Enterprise*), and even some little jelly-like beads known as chocolate tube slime, I knew I would soon have to return to the workaday world where few would share my enthusiasm for mushroom adventuring.

In fact, as I walked down the hill, stopping to feast on the blueberries and blackberries along the way, looking off to the sea and the hard blue clear horizon, I again wondered why all this mushroom gazing had made me feel better. I hadn't ingested any hallucinogenic psilocybin mushrooms or even tasted any fragrant chanterelles. Somewhere far off, men in suits were meeting in windowless rooms carving up the world and deciding which country is worth invading next. At this moment I could neither halt nor hinder their progress. Over the last two summers I had ingested a fair amount of history as part of my research and writing and that same world had remained much as it had been before I ate my fill.

Man, woman and boletus were still pretty much the same as they had been in 1919, 1749, or even during the time of Christ. Nobody was working the math anymore trying to figure out how to produce the greatest amount of happiness for the greatest number of people. In fact, maybe such a pragmatic plan inevitably meant that the minority would suffer in some way in order for this to happen. But, unlike Heidegger, I would refuse to be the puffball, the fibre head or the boletus that defined who he was by the inevitability of his corporeal demise. Instead, I would try to stand a little straighter and head directly into the cool northwest wind. I would walk the narrow, winding path back into my own life and the scheduled days ahead wondering if I too was created by lightning or at least some brilliant, epiphanic flash of a hundred thousand volts that put me here to make the most of the days I had allotted before they ran out.

August 26

Raven Paradox

It's August 26th, 8:12 a.m. I am sitting on Stoney Beach where the Lawrencetown River pours into the sea. The tide is high so there is a truce between the sea and the river. I am here in my "office" of sand and sea with notebook in hand. If I keep the right frame of mind, I am free and alone and the world of responsibilities is far away in time and geography. It's almost like holding my breath.

Before I can begin, I must remember something about this place. Straight out to sea from here, I once pulled in the drowned woman who had been carried to her death by a fierce outgoing river current while swimming at Stoney Beach. This is, after all, a river mouth and as the tide gets lower, the water travels with immense power back out to sea. I tried to save her. I swam her ashore but I was too late. I did my best. I brought her back. I had my first true taste of death as I put my mouth to hers, failing to breathe life back into her – this young woman and mother of small children.

This all happened sixteen years ago. It is a marker in my life. A corner turned. A sign posted. Once beyond that point you can never go back again, back to a kind of naïveté, that warm illogical illusion that we are all immortal and life goes on forever.

Now the air is still, tiny waves plop on the sand, some slapping hard and loud even though they are only a few inches in height. The sand is a hieroglyphic text of bird tracks. Now that I am stationary and not making loud noises or ambitious gestures, the shore birds are back. I am the only human among a great crowd of plovers. I know these to be semi-palmated plovers, although I haven't been able to figure out the meaning of the name or whether there are "fully" palmated plovers out there. These are beautiful little long-legged seabirds that run like cartoons characters and hang out in packs eating tiny sea insects. If they have anything at all to say, it sounds like two-wi-lee to my ear. When one gets scared and flies, they all fly. Plovers don't strike me as highly individualistic.

They are probably fine when there is no danger but even a hint of danger and they become very skittery. Perhaps with good reason. Their cousins, the much paler and fragile piping plovers, described as being "the colour of dried sand," are on the endangered species list. They nest in the sand dunes and grasses and are much disturbed by dogs and people. My daughter is part of a campaign to save the piping plovers and later she will hand me a postcard that I am supposed to mail to the prime minister. On one side is a healthy baby plover chick and alongside of it a dead one. In both English and French it says, "Plovers need beaches to survive. ATVs don't." And on the back is a letter to Jean Chrétien that reads in part, "Every year the piping plover's status becomes more precarious. All terrain vehicles operating illegally on beaches are crushing nests and chicks and pushing the species to extinction."

I like to envision Mr. Chrétien reading things like this and reacting immediately to the crisis. "Gosh darn," he will say. "We must save the plovers immediately." I am sure such things are still possible in Canada.

If this postcard works, we could advance to another directive to all world leaders in an effort to save the human race from extinction. Instead of ATVs, we get run over by greed and hatred. The two create a loud and destructive four-wheeler and usually an adolescent boy or someone who has not emotionally matured is at the wheel, hell-bent.

So it is getting near the end of summer, my summer at least, the end of my tenure as writer-in-residence of summer. My work might appear dull to anyone watching me. *Why is he sitting on a beach in the morning alone with books and notebooks and nothing else but clouds and cormorants and schizophrenic plover-kind to keep him company? What is he doing?*

The answer is this: he is getting back to essentials. Setting free the past, settling into the high water mark of here and now. There are clouds and cormorants above and off to the southeast, and what's left of Fox Point on the other side of the river at Conrad's Beach. Not much is left of what was once a solid spit of land with a gravel road and a community of fish shacks. Now it's just a ridge of rockweed-covered stones at low tide. So goes Fox Point. So goes all of us. But no grieving.

The plovers decide en masse that the beach buffet must be better over at Conrad's so they depart with lightning speed to the east. All that is left on Stoney is a writer and three large gulls. One herring gull ambles my way and drops down as if sitting on a nest about four feet away. The others follow him until I realize I am "surrounded," sitting epicentre of a triangle of three resting gulls. One begins to make sounds that sound very reminiscent of a cat meowing. Another performs the classic laughing gull signature although this is not the true laughing gull with the black head and darker body. Most folks just call these creatures sea gulls and they are alternately adored and detested. I'm wondering if one of my companions here is the same gull that attacks his own image in my second-storey window at home. The closest gull suddenly seems to have some commentary on the morning, announcing, hi-ya, hi-ya, hi-ya while the others remain mute.

I expect that these are the gulls of summer who have been spending too much time on the hot crowded beach with human bathers. They have been fed popcorn, potato chips and Cheesies and are hoping me to be so generous. They're out of luck on that count.

While Nova Scotia is the summer home of the herring gull, it is also the winter home of the Iceland gull and other arctic birds like the black-legged kittiwake and one of my favourite winter surfing companions, the dovekie, who seems to enjoy the company of a fellow life form bobbing up and down among the cold winter waves.

Missing this morning are ravens. The only raven noted so far was one hovering by the side of the road on the headland, making a study of a dead skunk that had been run over by a car on the curve of the road and that now perfumed the neighbourhood. The absence of ravens reminds me of something I came across recently in Robert Martin's philosophy book: "the raven paradox." I had high hopes for what the raven paradox might be, thinking that other more sophisticated thinkers than me had come up with a view of the world based on raven behaviour.

My own generalized raven theory for my travels goes like this:

One raven from home: a good omen;
Two ravens from home: the journey has begun;
Three ravens from home: I am on the right path;
Four ravens from home: there is something to be
discovered at every step;
Five ravens from home: you've come this far, you
should keep going;
Six ravens from home: test yourself, test a belief, and don't
settle for easy answers;
Seven ravens from home: far enough, now find
your way back.

The raven paradox, as it turned out, was more a matter of logic than metaphysics. Professor Martin begins with the notion that "All ravens are black." And this should be the same thing as saying, "All non-black things are non-ravens." But I can't quite see the value in knowing that a red rose is a non-raven. I don't quite see how this "paradox" advances human thought. Carl Hempel, a member of the so-called Vienna Circle of the 1920s and '30s formulated it. That circle also included luminaries with names like Schlick, Carnap and Godel who collectively set in motion something known as logical positivism.

The logical positivists (did their wives call them that? I wonder) decided that if something was not verifiable, it must be nonsense. Ethics, for example, was bullshit since you couldn't "prove" it. This seems ironic, since many of the Vienna circle ended up on the run from Hitler who thought he could prove anything with mere physical might.

The tide has risen some despite my certainty that it was already high tide. A thing is assumed to be true until evidence proves it to be otherwise? Choyce's Law. I now believe I am as smart as any man in the Vienna Circle. But a renegade moment of doubt suddenly prompts me to believe I am the opposite. I know almost nothing at all. The gulls and I sit here in some kind of opposition. We are not the Vienna Circle but we are the Lawrencetown Triangle. They are interested in potential Cheesies. I am interested in the potential mystery of everything around me. How far into the morning will this lead me before I must turn back home?

The gulls appear sleepy and I am wondering again about that red dot on their large yellow bills. It appears to be blood but is not and I've seen it on most of the gulls who cavort around here. Some evolutionary reason, I am sure. Maybe it makes them appear more threatening, more bloodthirsty. I once saw a granddaddy herring gull swoop and swallow seven baby ducks one after the next as my daughter and I canoed to save them. I know they can be nasty brutes. So maybe some deserve the blood spot. But not these Cheesie gulls with their high cholesterol level and propensity to poke around in garbage cans.

I'm of the opinion this quiet morning that modern philosophy has sucked some life out of the planet. I myself sometimes prefer the ancients. Heraclitus, for example, who lived in Ephesus during the fifth century, surmised that everything was made of fire and in a constant state of change. Sometimes known as Heraclitus the Obscure, he observed that all things were also related to each other. It was just that everything kept changing from one thing to another. In a way, each and every thing in the world was being consumed and transformed. My morning, my summer, my life. Like Fox Point I was eroding. But at the same time, the essence of my being was being distributed – to where I know not – but inside me was fire, I am sure. A small flame of a man sitting on the beads of sand by the shore of the great waters beneath the infinite sky. Thank you Heraclitus. To heck with Carl Hempel and the rest of the dullards in the Vienna Circle.

Henry Miller stated the obvious when he observed that writing was a form of discovery but he also had the wisdom to take it one step further, stating the goal of a writer: "He takes the path to become the path," and later, "only one good reader is necessary." More gratitude on my part for that. One good reader is all it takes. Are we there yet?

Friedrich Nietzsche, who said many foolish things in his time, reminisced about a place he loved – Portofino, on the coast of Italy. For him it was a "small forgotten world of happiness," a good phrase that also fits the psychological place I go to on good days when I am allowed to write and discover. Sadly, I once travelled to Portofino late in the twentieth century and there were great traffic jams getting in, parking problems, too many tourists and many foul smells. Once you lose places like Portofino, can Lawrencetown and Halifax be far behind?

I've willed the tide to come no further and the moon is satisfied with its coaching of the sea. Slippage from here on. The beach will increase its real estate and the plovers will certainly want to celebrate whatever low tide leaves on the dinner table.

When "small forgotten worlds of happiness" are remembered, it is often with a sense of longing – longing for something that is long gone. My own life was once built on a platform of longing that eventually collapsed and left me swimming in a murky sea of despair. I knew the proper strokes, but I was not a strong swimmer. However, I did understand the overwhelming power of a current racing away from land. You could never get back ashore by swimming against it. The only possible salvation was to swim across it until you were out of its grip, and even then, it was a long swim ashore to solid ground.

Across the sea from here is the Sahara desert. Nova Scotia was once part of the continent we now call Africa. There is evidence of glaciers beneath those desert sands south and east of here. Strange to think of Morocco once right here at my doorstep. But then the world was a different place. India was an island. Landmasses collided like bad drivers in heavy traffic. Continents swirled and jockeyed for position on the surface of the earth. Seas surged over lands and then retreated.

Our sun is five billion years old and has another five billion to go. It will become bigger, hotter. Seas will boil and then evaporate and soon the earth's atmosphere will burn off. Then our sun will become a red dwarf. We will all be long gone by this point and won't be in the galactic neighbourhood to see it shrink to the size of a planet, as it becomes a white dwarf and then, ultimately, goes out.

I walk now towards the narrow river that parts the sands, dividing Stoney Beach from Conrad's Beach. The water has already begun to flow out to sea. I pick up a single stone, always comforting, as if that's all that's needed to get by for one more day on the dying planet. In the distance on the Conrad shore, a woman has appeared with two large dogs. The dogs are running and she is dancing or exercising, I can't tell which, waving her arms around in high circles as if signalling maybe, or fanning an ember that she hopes will spark into flame.

August 30

Simplicity and Subwoofers

My brother's sons spend a lot of money on their cars and trucks. They own one or two of each and go to great lengths to "improve" them.

Bradley, for example, has a 1987 Monte Carlo that is burgundy. It boasts several illegal options including, my favourite, neon lights that glow on the undercarriage of the car. Why it is illegal to have neon lights that shine on the road beneath you is unclear to me but the law says this is a thing a young man should not do. He also applies a kind of coating to all his windows to make them dark – too dark to suit the law and that is illegal too. Dark inside, road lit up underneath the car while parked or driving.

The stereo system – amplifier array and subwoofer box – takes up most of the trunk where people used to store things like spare tires and tools and stuff to take to the beach. Now it's all subwoofer and 300-watt amplifier. The amplifier is in a Plexiglas display case that also has its own neon lighting.

Bradley's next big gift to his car – and I'm not sure if it is illegal – will be to remove the door handles. He doesn't like the look of cars with door handles. Instead, he will open the doors with a hand-held remote control device. Myself, I would not trust the hand-held remote control device. I don't even like power windows.

I like the old-fashioned stuff: crank down the window by hand, open the door with the grip of thumb and forefinger. Call me what you will.

Of course, Bradley has a remote starter for his car so he can start it up or, for that matter, turn it off, while he is inside watching a rental DVD movie on the family's big screen TV. He's also done a number of expensive, incomprehensible things to the engine of his Monte Carlo that makes it suck more gas, roar louder and go faster. I don't know what else he has installed in his car because I'm afraid to ask. But I'm sure whatever it is, it is expensive and will sooner or later be deemed by the law to be illegal.

In the garage sits a 1971 GM truck that Bradley has been tearing apart and putting back together since he was fifteen. He's now twenty-one. It's never been out of the shop since that time because of all the grinding of rust, sanding, repainting, rechroming, etc., etc. It is a lifetime project, Bradley says, and he is attempting to reconstruct the truck so that it is "perfect." I've warned Bradley of the pitfalls of perfection – my belief that it is unattainable whether you're talking about trucks, art, relationships, writing or democracy. Bradley says he only knows about trucks and on that count he thinks I'm wrong.

I once owned a 1957 Chevy station wagon when I was seventeen and while it was not perfect – I had dented it driving it around my yard before I was street legal – it came close. It had a 289 cubic inch engine that had been bored out to a 302. This was not a muscle machine in those days but anything that had been bored out had a cachet about it. It wasn't even particularly fast, but it got me where I was going. It had roof racks for me to strap on my nine-foot-six inch Greg Noll slot-bottom surfboard. I had a bored out 302 Chevy wagon and a slot bottom. There wasn't much else a guy needed back then but a wetsuit and a girlfriend. Eventually I had those as well.

I suppose this is evolving into me writing about simplicity and complexity because I woke up today feeling my life was too complicated, again. There are various wolves (and subwolves) at my door; many of them I have seen before. Some I will train to eat out of my hand; others will come back to haunt me at night. I remind myself this morning that at least I am keeping out of trouble. I have not gotten arrested like James Brown, the godfather of soul, whose songs used to play on the radio of my Chevy. James Brown was arrested at fifteen for stealing clothes out of people's parked cars. He spent three years in prison for that. He committed some other crimes after he was famous, one involving taking a shotgun into a building he owned in an attempt to intimidate whoever had used his private toilet there.

Later, James Brown's songs were replaced by Crosby, Stills and Nash tunes in my Chevy and I console myself that I did not go the route of David Crosby – consuming unfathomable quantities of drugs and toting guns, running from the law until 1986 when he turned himself in.

Even Sophia Loren spent some time in prison for tax evasion. Sophia Loren had been my favourite Italian actress when I was seventeen.

But my 1957 Chevy station wagon was stolen from me while I was in the movies at the Moorestown Mall watching Stanley Kubricks's *2001: A Space Odyssey*. It was like the end of an era. The end of innocence. The end of simple pleasures and youth. So here in the year 2003, I reflect on the lost car, lost youth and the years between watching the movie and living the actual year. This reflection made me come to the conclusion that I had made my life overly complicated and vowed to simplify things. But, as August Strindberg once said about growing older, "It's not nice but at least it's interesting."

This reflection on simplicity, complexity, aging, cars and Sophia Loren brings me back to write about Douglas's car. Douglas is Bradley's younger brother. He's nineteen. He owns a new white truck with a front seat and a backseat. There's a cap over the back of the new white truck and, as far as I can tell, he's never hauled anything in the back. When I was growing up, my grandfather had a truck that hauled barbed wire, or manure for the fields, or firewood, or lumber or corn stalks. Dirt sometimes. We did haul dirt from one location to another location on the planet because this was part of our business in those days. A truck was for hauling stuff. But not Doug's truck. It was new and white – a terrible colour for a truck – and, like his brother's Monte Carlo, you could start it up from inside the house and protect it with an electronic anti-theft system.

The truck only hauls Douglas himself from his house to the Best Buy store where he installs high wattage car stereo systems. Douglas is highly revered among his peers for his ability to make speaker boxes for subwoofers and his ability to change a Ford Taurus radio into a CD player in ten minutes or less.

But Doug's real claim to fame is his 1985 Ford Escort, an unlikely status car. Doug's specialty is not muscle machine but sound machine. He competes with other like-minded young men at car shows – not for speed, but for volume. Quality of sound, oddly enough, does not count that much. Just volume.

Anything taken to extreme, in my mind, is at once heroic and absurd. Stupid is another word that comes to mind but, in truth, I admire Doug's quest for volume. Remember, this is a legitimate area of knowledge and expertise: car sound equipment.

My '57 Chevy had an AM radio. No FM. It had one front speaker in the dashboard and I thought I had died and gone to heaven when I installed two extra speakers in the back. They were woofers, this in the days prior to subwoofers. (How low can you go?) After the Chevy was stolen I would own other cars with eight-track players and FM radios but none would sound as good as those installed speakers in the Chevy when the Shirelles were singing, "Dulang dulang dulang. He's so fine," coming to me personally across the airwaves from WIBG radio in Philadelphia. The DJs name was Hi Lit.

It was a warm May evening in my brother's front yard when Bradley showed me his Monte Carlo and turned on the undercarriage neon lights. It lit up the grass beneath the car with an otherworldly purple glow. Then Douglas arrived home from his job at Best Buy. He too wanted to show off his masterpiece: the '85 Ford Escort. The Ford Escort had duct tape holding the front windshield together. The car itself was black and unassuming – somebody's mother's car that used to drive kids to Scouts. A car for errands and groceries. I didn't get it.

Then Douglas opened the door. The inside of the car had been stripped bare. Nothing on the doors, or ceiling, or floor or door panels. The seats had been removed and in place of the driver's seat was a cinder block.

"You have to be able to drive it to the competition," Douglas explained. "You can tow it to the car show but once there you have to be able to drive it to the actual site to compete." That explained the luxury of the cinder block driver's seat perfectly. "And it has to run. The engine has to be running during the competition."

At that time, I still didn't understand the nature of the competition. "You're competing for the best sound system, right? The best sounding audio equipment?" I asked.

"No," he answered. "You don't get it, do you, Uncle Les? Not the best, the loudest."

Stanley Kubrick had failed to predict this in his legendary film. He had assumed we would have monoliths communicating to us from a moon circling Jupiter. He missed the mark by a country mile. We would have, in this brave new century, young men competing with stripped-down cars for the loudest sound system.

"You can't actually be in the car when the sound system is on," Douglas explained. "You have to turn it on by remote control."

Everything was remote control in their world. Everything was turned on or off from a distance. Maybe pretty soon, everything would be that way.

Langhorne, Pennsylvania, was one of those places grown men took teenage sons on weekends to "watch" competitions between volume gurus like Douglas to see who had the loudest sound system.

"What happened to the windshield?" I asked.

"The sound system shattered the glass," Douglas answered, trying not to sound like he was bragging.

Even his brother Brad was smiling, truly proud of the feat of his little brother. "Grandpop said we'd crack the windshield and he was right." Grandpop was my father, a man who had survived World War II and other global calamities and had probably long since given up trying to understand the complexity of human nature that led to Doug's current passion. Of course, my father had lost a high percentage of his hearing working around big machines and diesel trucks all his life. He and my mother sit in front of Peter Jennings each night hearing the news at a frightening volume, so I guess you could say that Doug and Bradley had grown up with volume and it was running in the family.

Doug lifted up the trunk of the Escort and inside was a 600-watt amplifier, enough wattage to satisfy Jimmy Hendrix in concert, and a pair of subwoofers that looked to be designed by NASA. Doug explained that at the competition, decimal meters were set up and everyone stood around the car with sound plugs in their ears. I nodded approval of any and all safety measures. "Since the winner is the one with the loudest system, you need to push the amp to its top volume."

"Makes sense to me."

"But you can only leave it on for maybe a second or two. Sometimes less."

"So you don't actually play like an entire song from a CD?"

"No. You just burp the system."

"You burp it?"

"Yeah. You just turn it on for a split second so it can register on the decibel meter."

"And the loudest wins?"

"Correct."

Douglas was fiddling with some wires in the trunk, reminding me of my own long-gone days of fiddling with wires to hook up my two back speakers in the Chevy. Doug explained that the car had several batteries hooked up because he needed lots of power to run the amp. I turned away for a moment to look up at the stars in the clear night sky. Suddenly I heard a sizzling sound and a bright arc shot out from the trunk of the Escort. Doug jumped back as a great plume of black smoke billowed out of the trunk. Like many an auto sound enthusiast before him, and despite his cult hero status in the decibel world, Douglas had apparently connected the wrong wires.

The smoke dissipated in the night air and Doug said he didn't think he'd be able to give me a demonstration tonight but it was nothing serious. Bradley kicked at the gravel in the driveway as Doug surveyed the melted wires in the trunk of the car. Aside from a distant dog barking, it was a quiet night in the early part of the century. The subwoofers had not been burped but they would sleep well that night, as would we all.

September 2

Galileo and Socrates

Some creature, a weasel perhaps or even a bobcat, killed my great friend Demosthenes last September. In another day or so, I would have moved his cage inside the house, up into my office, for the winter but I thought it best that he have as much "outside" time as the season would allow, as much natural life as a somewhat crippled blue jay could experience.

It didn't seem fair that Demosthenes had survived this long and grown to love pencils as toys and fax machines as entertainers. He had enjoyed his games of hiding pebbles and paper clips too, but then was taken by the needs of the wild kingdom.

This summer, the injured animals did not find their way into my home until early July. First, Pamela's friend Trish brought over a baby pigeon that had been in the parking lot of the McDonald's where she worked down by Halifax Harbour. It was the most ordinary of pigeons and had feathers but was not ready to fly. It was starving, having refused to eat the pieces of hamburger buns offered, and the bird was probably not fully weaned from its mother.

We force-fed it with water and cat food using a syringe (without the needle). It sounds ridiculous but that's the way to do it. Diluted cat food will save them. The little pigeon was devoid of personality but that quickly changed. Eventually I named it Galileo, in hopes that a lofty name would give him some lofty ambition and he'd seek the heavens. This bird, like Demosthenes, had some kind of wing injury or deformity and I expected he would never fly but I would not give up on that possibility altogether.

Hot on the heels of Galileo's arrival, Sunyata brought home another baby grackle from the rehab centre. He was the only grackle to survive from a handful that had come in when their nest had been destroyed and parents killed. He too had some kind of problem – feathers not coming in properly, a droopy wing. He squawked loudly whenever a person appeared; he wanted to be fed the pasty cat food and he wanted to be fed often. He was quite demanding.

Both had their cages on my back porch and both were brought into the sunroom at night. Galileo recovered quickly and regained his natural high-pitched frantic piping on his own behalf when he wanted to be fed. Smarter than the grackle who had not acquired his own name yet, the pigeon was soon wolfing down cracked corn and millet from my hand and batting his wings with enthusiasm while the grackle squawked on, demanding, demanding. Make no mistake. This was an ordinary grackle. I'm not saying he was exotic – not a boat-tailed grackle or a great tailed grackle, just a grackle – the "common" grackle, as they say in Peterson's book, *Quiscalus quiscula*. I decided to call him Socrates to give him a modicum of sophistication.

If Socrates were to survive to maturity, he would be a mid-sized kind of blackbird with that iridescent sheen – possibly purple or even bronze. The grackles I have seen have always been furtive-looking, nervous birds with darting eyes and spindly black legs. They acted as if they were stealing birdseed from a feeder even if it was offered freely. Peterson says that their single, one-note voice goes "chuck" or "chack." He even suggests that their "song" is "a split rasping note." This was the bird I had invited to live in my home.

"A split rasping note" is probably only one step better than his cousin, the brewer's blackbird whose "song" is "a harsh wheezy, creaking quee-ee or ksh-ee." My hope was that Socrates would quiet down after a while or that I could train him out of his "musical" inheritance.

Although he was in no way cuddly or cute or any of the things you might find endearing in a species, he was what he was and I was hoping he could teach me a thing or two. I discovered that he is related to some fine species since he was in the family *Icteridae*. His cousins are the red-winged blackbird who can gurgle "konk-la-ree" or even "o-ka-lay," bobolinks with their cheerful "pink, pink" oratory or simple outright statement of their own species name: "bob-o-link, bob-o-link." And Socrates' other cousin, the eastern meadowlark, has a song described as "two clear slurred whistles, musical and pulled out."

I was hoping Socrates could possibly learn these or other delightful bird sounds from the birds visiting my back porch to scavenge for overflow birdseed from the two recuperating birds.

One of my favourite personal myths is that caring for injured creatures builds up some kind of goodwill that will protect the caregiver and his family. I have believed this for a long time and, although it seems scientifically unsound, it makes me feel better about the world in general.

Those ravens by the highways are there keeping an eye on me, making sure I am safe, because I nursed one of theirs back to health and taught him to fly. (That was the semi-famous raven, Jack, named for Jack Kerouac). This is why they are along the highways or in the forests when I am lost, wandering compassless among the trees until I find a path back home. They are keeping an eye on me. They will keep an eye on my children. You would have a hard time persuading me that this is not so even though it sounds crazy enough.

So, two recovering birds on a back porch or in the sunroom establish some kind of force field that will protect my house and my family. I'm not saying that if a robber enters in the night, Socrates the grackle will wake Galileo and together the two of them will pluck out the robber's eyes. No, I'm not saying that. It works in some other more mystical and inexplicable way. If I care for a thing without expectation of any reward, that very act of caring sets in motion cosmic machinery that will return the favour.

"An act of kindness is better than a fat pie," says an old Russian proverb. And William Wordsworth, with his spirit buoyed by those light lofty birds of the Lake District, wrote of "That best portion of a good man's life, / His little, nameless, unremembered acts / Of kindness and of love." And so I slept more soundly at night believing – or wanting to believe – that Socrates and Galileo were keeping the force field in place for a while at least.

Neil Campbell and Janet Reece's massive university textbook with the blatant title, *Biology*, states, "Many social behaviours are selfish, meaning they benefit the individual at the expense of others, especially competitors." This explains a lot of things that have caused me grief and disappointment over the years. Birds do this, Campbell and Reece say, and so do people. "Superior foraging," for example, will mean that other less skilled foragers are deprived. I am reminded of my days in graduate school where I did not forage as well as some of my earnest classmates. I could not wrestle the meaning out of a line by T.S. Eliot as well as they could; I could not root out the purpose of writing an entire essay on the punctuation of John Milton.

In my own writing, however, I try to forage meaning out of everything that happens. I look for the matrix that links one thing to the next. The grackle informs me about the stock market, if I can only read the subtext; Galileo foretells the future of space travel. If I can retrain two injured birds to fly, will a trip to Mars be far off?

But then this. Reece and Campbell ask of us, "How then can we explain observed examples of what appears to be altruism or unselfish behaviour?" How indeed.

Take the Belding ground squirrel from the American West. If he sees a predator like a hawk or a coyote, he sets off his own predator alarm, a high shriek that warns his family and friends but draws attention to himself and makes it more likely that he himself ends up as lunch for his enemy.

Bees seem altruistic, although they don't get much credit for it. No one thinks of them as "kind." No bee has received a wall plaque or award for its selflessness. The so-called naked mole rats of Africa are another example. They are mostly blind and live together in underground colonies of as many as 250 of their clan. A queen is usually "married" to three males, or kings. Naked and blind, they have mole rat orgies and reproduce more offspring. The unlucky others forage for food for the colony and for the royalty and gladly fend off snake predators, often getting killed in the process. And yet again, no one is handing out medals to these little heroes.

Down by my garden, the willets, those long-legged marsh dwellers of the sandpiper family, flit around in the evenings while I'm picking peas or trying to give a pep talk to my discouraged tomato plants. The willets have a nest nearby in the high grass and mistake me for an enemy. They announce their name loudly: "Willet, willet, willet" or if they take to higher flight, they actually pipe, "Wee, wee, wee." If I so much as look in the direction of their ground nest, they dart towards me and draw attention to themselves. They want me to chase them and not disturb their nest. They have wings and I have none, but they know my species can be dangerous. We can crush their babies with roaring ATVs or load shotguns and blast them to smithereens. So the parents do the selfless thing, their altruistic thing, because protecting your young is what you must do.

Once, in New Brunswick, I was walking in a Fundy marsh and another long-legged shorebird detected I was headed towards her nest. (Or his nest, maybe.) The bird flew close and lay down on the grass, pretending it was injured, luring me away from whatever she wanted to protect.

At the Paris Peace Conference of 1919, many members of various national delegations drew up plans to punish the Germans, saying they deserved to be beaten down into poverty and servitude for having inflicted such suffering on all of Europe and beyond. Yet others, and Woodrow Wilson was one of them, believed that the only way to prevent future wars was to treat the defeated nation with dignity and compassion. A compromise was reached but, unfortunately for the world, whatever compassion was in it for the Germans was watered down with revenge and insistence on reparations.

The victors parcelled up the colonies of the losers and grabbed the wealth available to them, as any good forager would do. The altruists had their say but their songs were drowned out by the hawks and eagles and other great birds of prey.

One fine fall day, trying to assist a Canada goose shot down by a hunter, Sunyata and I were standing in the side yard trying to feed the goose when a harrier hawk dove out of the sky and grabbed one of my pigeons. This small hawk flew off with my pigeon in its talons as Sunyata and I chased it. Eventually, he dropped his prey and, breathless from the chase, we gathered up the fallen bird and took it home, nursing yet another bird back to health. The goose died but it would seem that the only reason we were there to save the pigeon was because we were attending the goose.

On my back porch today, the sun is bright and Galileo blinks at the light. Socrates, the grackle, is in conversation with the empty sky. My various wetsuit boots and gloves are drying in the morning breeze. The Bermuda High has moved off and with it the fog. The return of sunshine to my coast is like the beginning of the renaissance. As the original Galileo Galilei would have noted, "Perchance, other discoveries still more excellent will be made from time to time by me or other observers."

September 9

Return to Wedge Island

Although it is not officially the end of summer, it is the end of my summer. Fall responsibilities of teaching, travelling, school visits, and publishing duties have already begun. This weekend brought us the first hurricane swell of the year. Fabian roared across Bermuda, lifting roofs from homes, pelting down buckets of rain. Then the storm headed north, veering east as is often the case and sparing Nova Scotia, leaving my roof still on my house.

But as the storm passed by, the waves rose in height and I surfed long enough to noodle the muscles of my arms and legs. The water remained oddly cold as it has all summer. The records have all been broken for cold water and fog on these shores. Surfing in Seaforth on Saturday, I admitted that I found it unnerving to be in the ocean at evening, as the fog grew more and more dense. Usually, a surfer can sit on his board and watch the wave approach, position himself for the best place to paddle and take off. But the fog would not allow that. So I sat tensely in the water with my friends as overhead hurricane-generated waves reared up in the distance. Catching a wave now required intuition and guesswork. And sometimes we were in the wrong place at the wrong time. Suddenly an overly ambitious monster of a wave would appear out of the gloom immediately upon us and thunder down. All I could do was abandon my leashed board and dive deep to let all that power pass above.

But in luckier moments, I would be in the right place at the right time. Then it was a full-muscled paddle to make the take off, drop down the face of the glassy wall and race across the wave, all with little to no visibility. You could see your hand in front of your face but that was about all. Each wave was a journey into the unknown and every nerve in your body was attuned to keeping ahead of the roaring, collapsing wave that was chasing you, preparing to gobble you up if you so much as hesitated for a second. And if you didn't kick out at the correct instant, you could find yourself pummelled onto the unforgiving shoreline, face-first, kissing boulders and rocks.

In K.C. Cole's book *First You Build a Cloud*, she points out, "The wave can separate itself from the original disturbance that created it and carry information far from its source... it can interact with other waves... it is not made of 'stuff.'" The role of the surfer, I would add, is to put himself in the way of the wave and tap into all that information, interact with all that travelling energy, become part of the story, become part of the hurricane itself in this case.

Catching that travelling encyclopaedia of watery power requires physical thrust but also an intuitive belief that it is indeed possible to become one with the wave, at least for a short while. We call it "riding" the wave but riding is a very weak verb. As far as I know, Albert Einstein never surfed but he understood the nature of energy in the form of waves. And at least a few of my fellow surfers would agree with Einstein's wisdom when he said, "There comes a point where the mind takes a leap – call it intuition or what you will – and comes out on a higher plane of knowledge."

With all of that information roaring at us from Hurricane Fabian, some of us left the sea with our heads stuffed to overflowing with knowledge and our knees wobbly with exhaustion.

It's two days later and the skies are clear, the sea has calmed itself and the hurricane, demoted to a tropical storm now, is moving towards Greenland. I learn on the news that three men have died south of Newfoundland, their bodies recovered by the Coast Guard. The victims were three Israeli citizens who had purchased a sailboat in Nova Scotia and were headed across the Atlantic towards England. For unknown reasons, they ignored the strong advice of other sailors ashore here who told them it would be foolhardy and deadly to leave port with a hurricane approaching. Fabian had pretty much performed as predicted and many of us had been tracking it on the Internet since it was spawned off the coast of east Africa. Although there had been survival suits on board, the Israeli men had not been wearing them when their bodies were found.

So now it is September ninth and I am close to completing my two-summer journey that has no final destination. I have decided to hike out to the headland that has the furthest reach out into the sea itself. Wedge Island is tethered to the mainland by a narrow ridge of rocks and is a difficult place to hike to at the best of times. I have misjudged the tides this morning. It's dead high tide. Each rock from here to the Wedge is itself an island. Waves slap up from both sides. But in the distance, the high narrow remnant of headland looks more appealing than ever, more necessary. So I begin my journey, gracelessly crawling and jumping from boulder to boulder, registering that the thin coating of green slime on the rocks makes foot and hand grips that much harder. I end up spider-like crawling on all fours, adventurous but cautious.

I watch the waves and must make my jump from rock to rock between the swells. A third of the way there I see that the necessary leap to the next boulder is more than I expected. I consider turning back but remind myself that as long as I don't slip and smash my head, the worst that will happen is that I'll spill into the sea, get cold and wet and maybe lose my copy of the *Dictionary of Philosophy* that I carry along for occasions like this.

My leap is successful, although my feet dip into the sea. Then further along, I realize that my luck at leaping will not hold. I take off my shoes, roll up my pants and step down into the shallows only to realize it's deeper than expected. My shoes, laces tied and strung over my shoulder fall into the water and are nearly carried away by a wave. I retrieve them and soldier on, crotch deep in the cold water of the North Atlantic.

I put my soggy shoes back on after much painful barefoot battles with barnacles and sharp rocks. Further on, in the lee of the high cliff of the Wedge Island headland, I take off my shoes and pants and set them on a boulder in the morning sun to dry. I sit and assess the situation. I notice my shoes have a name: Franklin, named for Ben or for the ill-fated arctic explorer, I wonder. My Franklins drain seawater as I beat my pants on rocks to help dry them, like women doing laundry in Third World countries. And then I wonder what an observer must think if he is holding up his binoculars back there on the mainland, seeing a shaggy-haired man in his underwear beating his pants on the rocks.

So I am here, sitting in my underwear in the sun on the cold rocks waiting for my pants and shoes to dry. I remember that I had been invited to a reception this morning with the Canadian consul of Los Angeles to learn about opportunities for selling film rights to American producers. But I opted for this instead and think myself lucky.

Instead of cursing my bad luck of high tide and wet cold clothes, I decide I am not so bad off. Many have it worse than I do. The tide may drop and it will be an easier trek home. In fact, I now have a kind of license to stay longer. The longer I tarry on the Wedge, the easier it will be to walk back to the mainland. The moon will do its work, the sea will follow its instructions and billions of gallons of water will move off somewhere else on the face of the planet.

I am almost giddy with my good luck.

I have personal history with this isolated place. I've brought my children here many times (on lower, safer tides) to walk among the nesting seagulls that lay their eggs atop the Wedge. We've returned to be among the dozens of gull chicks – great fluff balls of bird who are tame and look nothing like the full-fledged gulls. And I've also been out here on the bleakest of December days as well, just to feel the sensation of being at sea, adrift from the mainland.

I bide my time well. Wedge Island will be gone within my lifetime. It is slowly but surely being swallowed by the sea. Each advancing Fabian or Isabella speeds up the demise of what were once farms and homes of fisherman.

The clarity of the morning allows me to see islands twenty miles or more down the coast from here. It is a bold blue day and I realize that for some reason not a single raven has appeared to me yet. There are gulls aloft and small leggy shorebirds but nothing else. I squint into the bright light and remind myself how limited our perception actually is. As K.C. Cole puts it, "The pupil is but a tiny porthole in a sea of radiation." That radiation is now helping to dry my jeans, my purple socks and my Franklin shoes. I can't see most of it. I'm limited to seeing light with a wave width between .00007 and .00004 centimetres.

I'm aware that my other senses are relatively dull as well. I sometimes can't tell extreme cold from extreme heat. I can't distinguish smells as expertly as my old dog Jody and I'm deaf to most of the range of sounds, noises and music going on around me. But these limitations have their advantages. Suppose, for example, I could pick up radio and TV signals organically. Imagine the racket that would be going on in my head even here on remote Wedge Island. I decide I'm okay to work with what I've got: eyes, nose, ears, tongue and goose-pimpled skin reminding me that the rising chill of the wind suggests I should get moving.

I shovel myself back into soggy jeans, and socks, and shoes and hike to the top of the headland and further out to sea. The baby seagull chicks have all been reared, taught to fly and have moved on. A few skeletons remain, their bones picked clean by their neighbours.

The gulls will find another roost when the Wedge has fallen into the sea. The glaciers made this place – gathered stone and soil, and in their retreat, left this lump of a headland for the sea to feast on until satisfied. The eighteenth-century Italian philosopher Giovanni Battista Vico saw civilization as much the same. He thought the natural progression of history, of civilization, was theocracy, aristocracy and democracy. As one eroded, the next phase evolved. An optimist, and a man whose ideas are not much in favour in this century, he believed it all to be part of some divine plan. First God is in charge, and then kings and eventually everyone has a piece of the power. I don't know what comes after democracy. Vico is tight-lipped on that one. Where does the headland go when it is gone? Its very soil is dispersed into the sea, I suppose. We are all in flux.

If the Dalai Lama were here hiking with me right now, he would probably remind me that the greatest potential for gain in your life comes about during times of greatest difficulty. We should not allow problems to discourage us or make us feel helpless. Cold and wet is not so bad for a man alone walking through a field of shoulder-high purple thistles.

Off to the west of here is Rat Rock and Shut In Island. Both look tame today but each is a lonely slab of rock that must take the full brunt of everything the sea can throw at it. A man who must have also been philosophical about discomfort and lonely places once lived on Shut In Island. In Allison Mitcham's *Offshore Islands of Nova Scotia and New Brunswick*, she writes of a man named Clairmont who had committed a murder in the United States and built a house on Shut In (or Chetigne Island as it was once called by the local Acadians). He lived alone and pretended to be mute and on very still nights, people on the mainland could hear him playing the violin. Some think he found pirates' treasure there and was rich but fearful of returning to the mainland lest he be caught and punished for his crime.

Another loner to have lived on Shut In was a Mr. Lloyd who worked as a pilot for sailing ships headed to Halifax Harbour. He resided in a stone house that he built on this isolated chunk of rock so he would have first crack at the traffic headed to Halifax. He'd see the ships before any other pilot and row out to them, guide them to port and then row back home to his lonely abode. His closest rival was a Mr. Leslie who lived on Wedge Island. Leslie sometimes made his way out through the rough seas to offer his skill as a pilot only to discover that Mr. Lloyd was already aboard.

Some people say there is a light seen at night on Shut In Island – a ghost light left by Mr. Lloyd. Others think it is just the moonlight reflecting on the surface of a small pond at the centre of the place. I kayaked to Shut In one fine summer day, followed by bull seals that tried to spook me by rising up and flopping down in the water like fat men doing belly flops in a pool. It was a paddle of maybe two miles and when I stepped ashore on the island I felt stunned and shaken. The mainland looked much further away than I expected.

Alone on an island at sea with the wind rising and only a tiny boat to make my return, I felt scared. No one even knew I had taken the journey. It was a whim. The waters around the island were reputed to have dangerous currents. I had felt their tug as I drew close. Shut In itself was a bit of a disappointment. If seagull shit was your passion, you would have been happier here than me. I know that guano was once highly prized and sailing ships carried Peruvian bird shit all the way from there to here to use as fertilizer and God knows what else. But I needed more than guano.

I calmed myself. I pretended to be a rational man while the maniac within played reruns of *Jaws* and *The Perfect Wave* and conjured sea beasts well known to frightened mariners of ages past.

I did not seek out the ghost of Mr. Lloyd that day but put the rational man and the maniac both into the little kayak and pushed off for home. The bull seals again rose up and crashed down behind me over and over, tempting me to turn quickly and tip, perhaps. But I kept my eye on the mainland and the hill that was my home, which from here seemed impossibly far away. I had overextended my reach. My arms were weak; the sun was doing funny things to me so I stayed focussed on one stroke of the paddle at a time. Dip east, dip west, and point the bow of the boat true north.

An Indian philosopher named Shantideva reminds his students to face difficulties squarely without allowing them to "paralyze" you. The 1866 *Oxford English Dictionary* notes an example of using "paralyse" as a figure of speech: "His pride paralysed his love." To paralyse can refer to rendering one into a state of helplessness. I am aware, as I sit on these Wedge Island stones today, facing both Rat Rock and Shut In Island, that I had been headed toward a kind of paralysis before I began my two-summer search. My internal kayak was drifting towards oblivion. I was paddling in proverbial fog. I didn't know where the mainland shore was and I didn't know which giant wave would next knock me from my board and leave me floundering in a cold, merciless sea.

Oddly enough, here and now, sitting, contemplating, doing nothing, I am in a state of grace, much the opposite of where I had been. The things that have saved me have been documented here and elsewhere and all deserve my gratitude. A quick inventory of what is filling up my senses right now includes the rust and gold coloured rockweed in the lagoon at my bare feet. The blue of the water itself. A sudden recognition that blue and gold together makes for a bold visual statement and a damned good one. Smooth stones are to be congratulated, as are the cormorants poised upon those slippery rocks, posing like archangels, drying their wings in the morning air. There are sea ducks, diving down for eelgrass, then bobbing up like toys, surfacing dry. (Who devised that miracle?)

Across the water from me, in the seaward pools of Rat Rock, are massive seals lying above water on the stone outcroppings. And they are singing. They really are. It is a haunting sound much like that of the howling north wind in winter. Perhaps that is where they learned the tune. It is a wail and a moan and one could call it "mournful" but that word does not fit this morning.

I am aware that the lowland Scots, hearing this very sound from the seals, believed it to be coming from spirits they called kelpies, who had horselike heads (as these seals do) and lured sailors and travellers into deep waters to drown. But I do not think the seals are singing to lure me to my death. The Irish men of the sea had their own tales of men alone in the Atlantic in small boats being comforted by female seals taking human form. They too had heard the singing and found it hopeful, not mournful.

For there is little to mourn today. In the clear pools, the periwinkles, tiny-shelled snails, go about their daily routine by the thousands. The green sea urchins, cousins to the starfish, crowd into the crevices of rock. In the water I spy sea lettuce, Irish moss, sponges, free flowing alaria, swarthy kelp and ever abundant rockweed. There are rock crabs scuttling below and their dead cousins seem to have strewn their carcasses on the drying seaweed along the high tide mark. (Wearing your skeleton on the outside does not insure survival.) Two flying dowitchers spitfire by me and another pair are on their heels – much more entertaining than the weekend air show of military fliers at Shearwater Air Base.

Watching the water, I am convinced now the tide is dropping and I will have an easier return home, possibly even a dry passage from this island back to the mainland. I head back, first walking the spine of smooth bedrock that looks like the back of a whale and onto more difficult ledges where the vertical slate looks like the compressed edges of pages in a book, a very thick volume. Hobbes perhaps, his *Elements of Philosophy* in which he suggests, "The train of thoughts, or mental discourse, is of two sorts. The first unguided, without design and inconstant... and the second is more constant: as being regulated by some desire, and design."

Hobbes favours the latter and I, for the time being, the first, although, in truth, if Thomas Hobbes were with me, I would propose an amalgam of both: unguided, without design, but filled with desire. The name of that desire is elusive but there is no ultimate need to catch a wild thing, kill it, nail it upon a board and name it for all to see how clever you are.

Sure enough, the moon has done its work. The sea has dropped well below the jutting rocks and I can walk the sea floor back to the mainland. Once I've shut down all my cautionary footwork on slippery stones, a pike of long brown kelp positions itself beneath me and I slide upon it, falling on my Hobbes and *Field Guide to the Birds*. Still on my back, I am staring at the sky and see that I've disturbed a bald eagle, apparently posted on the shoreward seawall, studying my return to land. He rises in the air and heads off to the Wedge. Maybe that's why he is here. He was waiting for me to leave the island where he prefers to abide.

And now I am still wet, tired, slightly chilled and philosophical. And the morning has passed without my notice of one single raven. The code has been broken.

I drive slowly home and see my first raven standing by the side of the causeway. There are two more ravens tearing open black plastic trash bags in front of the house advertising a home business: "Aesthetician," the only one on Causeway Road.

A fourth raven is at the stop sign, high atop an electric pole. Ravens five and six fly across the road near the base of Porters Lake, near where the summer kayaker died. But there is no seventh raven anywhere to be seen. I almost wonder if I should keep driving. But I am cold and weary and my car wants its driveway. I pull to the top of the driveway and get out, stand there squinting into the morning sun. The grackle, Socrates, who lives in the cage on the open back porch, is looking at me with that curious look. *There you are. Where have you been? What are you all about? When are you going to feed me more grub worms or slapped mosquitoes or peas from your garden?* He tilts his head one way and then the other, waiting.

I hear him before I see him. Loud and raucous. An old raven, scraggly even, sitting in the high spruce tree above the house. He's watching me, reminding me I'm at my destination. Having travelled seven ravens from home only to discover that I am at my own back door.